Buggy Wheel RESTAURANT
COOKBOOK · VOL. II

Pies, Breads & Baked Desserts

A COLLECTION OF RECIPES
from EMPLOYEES
and FAVORITE HOUSE RECIPES

Esther Mishler and
Joel & Kim Mishler, Publishers

Barbara Bontrager, Recipe Coordinator

Buggy Wheel Restaurant
160 Morton Street, Shipshewana, Indiana

Book Design and Editor: Martha K. Stern
Cover Illustration: Bread Box Bake Shop by Dee Birkey

© Copyright Buggy Wheel Restaurant 1990
Buggy Wheel Restaurant, P.O. Box 353, Shipshewana, IN 46565

ISBN 0-927644-14-2

Contents

Welcome 4

Meet Our Family 5

Bread Box Bake Shop 8

Menno-Hof 10

About the Recipes 13

HOUSE RECIPES 15

BREADS 25

PIES 44

CAKES 63

COOKIES 80

DESSERTS 102

Index 117

To Order Cookbooks 127

Welcome...

We here at the Buggy Wheel Restaurant are pleased to bring you this second volume in our cookbook series. We hope you are enjoying the first one, <u>Main Dishes & Vegetables</u>. As you prepare and serve something freshly baked from these pages, may you have times of warm fellowship with family and friends.

Our cookbooks are an answer to requests for recipes from our restaurant guests. We are appreciative of our guests' interest. Thus we hope these cookbooks are helpful to one and all.

Many of our most popular dishes are prepared from recipes created and developed by our employees. Consequently, we owe much recognition and appreciation to our cooks and staff. Some have been with us almost since opening day. The greatest measure of Buggy Wheel's success is due to a dedication to quality and service from our entire staff.

Come, visit with us soon. While you are here, you will find much to enjoy in Shipshewana. Included in these pages is some information about Menno-Hof, the Mennonite-Amish Visitors Center, one of the ways in which our community shares its heritage with you. We look forward to meeting you and getting to know you and your family.

The MISHLERS ---

Joel & Kim

Esther

Meet Our Family

Joel and Kim Mishler and Esther Mishler are co-owners of the Buggy Wheel Restaurant. However, every member of their immediate family has contributed in many ways to the success and building of the Buggy Wheel.

The family of Gerald and Esther Mishler spent their growing up years on the farm. From the time of their marriage in 1956 until 1980, Gerald and Esther and their four children worked together on the farm. In 1969, the family moved onto Esther's childhood farm. Their experiences on the farm developed qualities that are evident in the Buggy Wheel Restaurant today.

A long-time dream of Gerald's was realized when the Buggy Wheel became a reality to the family in 1981. He saw his family's work in the restaurant as another way to instill his belief that "being successful in life involves being the best that you can be at whatever you are doing."

Entering the field of insurance and eventually purchasing the agency in 1970, Gerald began a successful business to support his growing family. The children had taken over much of the work on the farm. At the time of his death in 1988, the agency office was located next door to the Buggy Wheel.

Esther brings many strengths to the Buggy Wheel--her love of cooking and baking, her skills in homemaking, her quiet support of others

that enables them to do their best. Her natural
way is to work behind the scenes, and she has
adapted to the business successfully. Esther,
along with Gerald, taught their children faith and
to work together in unity with family and peers,
developing in them traits that have strengthened
them.

Oldest son, Jerold, his wife Laura, and their
three children still live and work on the family
farm just outside Shipshewana. He is keeping the
continuity of the farm life and carrying on the
family's support and involvement in 4-H through
raising champion lambs. Jerold also spent many
hours at the Buggy Wheel as he was the head baker
when the Bread Box Bake Shop first opened in 1985.

The two youngest in the family are daughters
Jennifer and Jane. Jennifer, a medical secretary,
is married and lives with her husband Jere in
Denver. Jane, the youngest, and her husband Dennis
are elementary school teachers in the area. Both
daughters worked in the Buggy Wheel during school
years, between college and career, capably using
their abilities waitressing, hostessing or wherever
else they were needed.

Joel, the second in the family, took over the
management of the Buggy Wheel in May, 1982 right
after graduation from Grand Canyon University in
Phoenix. Joel appreciates the fact that his father
encouraged him as an equal partner from the
beginning, thus ensuring that Joel's success was
his own.

The newest member of the Mishler family is Kentucky native Kim Ray Mishler, Joel's wife. They met through the hospitality industry as Kim worked for a restaurant supply company in Louisville. The two were married in October, 1989. Kim, the office manager, works in well in the family businesses which require sun-up to sun-down involvement.

You have met the Mishlers in these pages. However, there are many more members in this family since the Mishlers feel that their family really includes all their employees, both past and present --The Buggy Wheel Family.

Since the restaurant opening, the Mishlers give credit to their employees saying that "they have made the place what it is by being the best they can be."

Bring your friends and family to meet and visit with our Buggy Wheel Family soon!

Bread Box Bake Shop

The Bread Box Bake Shop is located in a charming setting behind the Morton Street Bed & Breakfast Home. The aroma of freshly baked bread beckons you to follow the curved brick walkways to the gingham curtained door. Rustic wood benches that encircle the shaded lawn invite you to linger while enjoying a freshly baked roll or plump cookie warm from the ovens.

When the ovens of the Buggy Wheel Restaurant could no longer keep up with the demand for take-home baked goods, the Bread Box was opened in 1985. Its ovens are filled with the delicious breads, pies and desserts that are served fresh daily in the Buggy Wheel. Guests can select from a generous variety and take home this same wholesome goodness remembered from days past.

Several kinds of bread, including apple-cinnamon, are baked into big crusty loaves to satisfy hearty appetites. Cream cheese brownies and peanut butter bars are melt-in-the-mouth good for company dessert or coffee breaks.

Almost everything from the Bread Box can be ordered by mail. Special made-to-order gift boxes are available year-round. Especially popular are old-fashioned tall, round cookie tins each holding a dozen of several varieties of Bread Box cookies. These country decorated tins are wonderful gifts for friends and business associates.

The bakers in the Bread Box use only fresh flours, eggs and seasonings in recipes created and kitchen-tested first in their own homes. They use traditional non-machine methods, kneading, shaping, rolling and cutting by hand. Every loaf of bread, cake and pie is "honest-to-goodness homemade" --by hand!

The staff of the Bread Box takes this commitment to heart. The bakers, some having been at the Shop since its opening, hand down this legacy of excellence to others. The Bread Box Bake Shop ovens turn-out only the best for guests to enjoy and to take home to share with their family and friends.

Menno-Hof

Menno-Hof, the Mennonite-Amish Visitors Center in Shipshewana is much like an Amish farmstead with its white two-story house and large red barn. The Center's name comes from the German word "Hof" meaning farmstead and "Menno" from Menno Simons, a leader of the early Anabaptists.

Visitors learn accurate information about this group of believers from which the area's Amish and Mennonites come. Menno-Hof opened in 1988 to tell the story of these peace-loving people, answering questions visitors have about present day lifestyles and faith practices of Amish and Mennonites.

Menno-Hof tells the story from the earliest beginnings of Anabaptists in 1525 to present day.

Today's Mennonites and Amish are strongly linked with who they were in the past. A people of diversity, they have strong beliefs that unite them in a worldwide fellowship.

The Center portrays this unity and diversity through multi-projector slide and audio presentations, pictorial displays, story telling, song, and re-creations of settings from their past and present.

Visitors begin their journey through the Center with an introduction to the Anabaptist movement by way of a multi-projector slide program.

The story of why and how Menno-Hof was built is told through video beautifully capturing the day by day progress of the building of the Center. Hundreds of Amish and Mennonites from the local area and across the country voluntarily worked together in a traditional "barn-raising." The huge structure was raised in six days using heavy oak beams fastened with knee braces and green oak pegs instead of modern-day iron nails and bolts.

Using this old technique for the framework of Menno-Hof illustrates the commitment of the Center to authenticity. Visitors experience this at every step of their journey through the Center.

In the Center's tornado theater, visitors experience the power of a tornado; for some it is almost too real. Mennonites and Amish who have a commitment to serving others are often involved in major cleanup following tornadoes and floods.

Helping those who are in need is a tenet of the faith of a people who in the past suffered much hardship because of their beliefs.

A 16th-century European courtyard, complete with working well, has been re-created to tell the story of how a simple clay pitcher of water led to a quiet people being chased from their homelands and imprisoned for their beliefs. Entering a dark dungeon, visitors have a real sense of being in that time and place.

A harbor, complete with harbormasters shack, and a 17th-century sailing ship tell of the Anabaptist migrations to America in their search for peace.

Anabaptists are a people of peace, one of the principles that unites these diverse people into a worldwide fellowship. The Center shares the story of a people committed to community, stewardship and simplicity.

On the last step of the journey through Menno-Hof, in the hush of a simple meetinghouse, visitors can witness the quiet faith that has sustained these people through the centuries.

Courtesy MENNO-HOF

About the Recipes . . .

This second Buggy Wheel Cookbook has more favorite recipes created in our own kitchens and some shared with us by family and friends. It is part of our heritage to fellowship with family and friends at mealtimes. Something warm from the oven often evokes memories of such times of fellowship. We hope you will enjoy baking from these recipes and will share with others.

We have tried to be as accurate as possible in writing down our recipes. Some of our ovens are non-electric and temperatures and time for baking may need to be adjusted. For all recipes, ovens should be preheated and pans prepared to prevent sticking depending on the type of pan. Unless specific directions are given, use standard methods for mixing and kneading. In recipes where sugar is used, use granulated or white sugar. Unless otherwise listed, use all-purpose flour.

The House Recipes included are just some of the favorites from our own Bread Box Bake Shop. Our staff bakes just like you do, preparing our baked goods one or two at a time. The "House Recipe" on the next page is one the Buggy Wheel staff has shared and would like to share with you.

May you, and those you share with, enjoy everything you bake from these recipes.

Barbara Bontrager

We do not give out all of our House Recipes—some are secrets. The following "House Recipe" is no secret, as we encourage all employees and staff to openly share with all our guests who enter our doors. Hopefully, everyone will like it so well, they will share with all mankind.

Happiness Cake

1 cup of good thoughts
1 cup of kind deeds
1 cup of consideration for others
2 cups of sacrifice
2 cups of well-beaten faults
3 cups of forgiveness

Mix thoroughly. Add tears of joy, sorrow and sympathy. Flavor with love and kind service. Fold in 4 cups of prayer and faith. Blend well.

Fold into daily life. Bake well with the warmth of human kindness and serve with a smile anytime. It will satisfy the hunger of starved souls.

WHITE BREAD   House Recipe

1/4 cup sugar   1/2 cup dry yeast
2 1/2 cups warm water (100 degrees)

Put in bowl and let set for 10 minutes or until the yeast is dissolved.

Add:

1 1/2 cups evaporated milk   1 cup lard, melted
3/4 cup sugar   1/4 cup salt
6 cups warm water   26 cups flour

Put in several cups of flour at a time, mixing well after each addition. When too stiff to stir, mix with hands. If the dough is still sticky, add more flour, kneading until dough is elastic.

Let rise 1 hour or until double. Divide dough into loaves. Shape loaves and place in greased 9x5x2 bread pans. Makes 12 (1 1/2 lb.) loaves. Let rise 1 hour in a warm place.

Bake at 350 for 25 to 30 minutes or until done. Brush tops of the hot loaves with melted butter.

COOK'S   Amount of flour needed may vary due to
 NOTE   humidity and type of flour.

BIG BRAN MUFFINS   House Recipe

5 cups flour
10 oz. raisin bran flakes
3 cups sugar
2 teaspoons salt
5 teaspoons baking soda

Combine dry ingredients and add:

4 eggs, well-beaten
1 cup vegetable oil
1 quart buttermilk
4 cups raisins

Mix well. Fill muffin pans 3/4 full. Bake at 350 for 15 minutes. Makes approximately 2 1/2 dozen.

COOK'S NOTE   Batter will keep in covered container in refrigerator as long as 6 weeks.

BLUEBERRY MUFFINS   House Recipe

1/2 cup shortening, softened
3/4 cup sugar
2 eggs, well-beaten
1 teaspoon nutmeg
2 1/3 cups flour
1/2 teaspoon salt
2 1/2 teaspoons baking powder
3/4 cup milk
1 1/3 cups blueberries

Beat shortening and sugar until light and fluffy. Beat in eggs. Add dry ingredients and milk. Fold in blueberries. Fill muffin pans 3/4 full. Bake at 350 for 15 minutes. Makes about 1 1/2 dozen large muffins.

PECAN PIE   House Recipe

4 eggs, well-beaten   1 teaspoon vanilla
1 cup brown sugar   1 teaspoon flour
1 cup white corn syrup   1 cup pecans (halves or
1/4 cup butter, melted   pieces)

1 9-inch unbaked pie shell

Mix together all ingredients, except pecans. Do not overbeat.

Spread pecans evenly in bottom of unbaked shell. Pour filling over pecans.

Bake at 400 for 20 minutes. Reduce heat to 300 and bake for another 10 to 15 minutes.

Cool pie completely before cutting.

PUMPKIN PIE   House Recipe

2 eggs, well-beaten   1 teaspoon cinnamon
1 1/2 cups pumpkin   1/2 teaspoon ginger
3/4 cup sugar   1/4 teaspoon cloves
1/2 teaspoon salt   1 2/3 cup evaporated milk

1 9-inch unbaked pie shell

Mix well all ingredients in order given. Pour into unbaked pie shell.

Bake at 375 for 50 to 55 minutes or until knife inserted in center comes out clean.

Cool before cutting.

RHUBARB CUSTARD PIE   House Recipe

2 eggs, well-beaten   1 cup evaporated milk
1 1/2 cups sugar   1 teaspoon vanilla
2 tablespoons flour   1/4 cup butter, melted
1/8 teaspoon salt   2 cups diced rhubarb

1 9-inch unbaked pie shell

Mix together all ingredients in order given. Pour into unbaked pie shell.

Bake at 400 for 10 minutes; then reduce heat to 325 and continue baking until set (approx. 30 minutes).

PINEAPPLE COOKIES   House Recipe

1 cup shortening
2 cups brown sugar
2 teaspoons vanilla
2 cups crushed pineapple,
   drained (reserve juice)

3 1/2 cups flour
2 teaspoons baking powder
1 teaspoon salt

Cream together shortening and sugar. Add vanilla. Stir in pineapple.

Sift dry ingredients together and add to pineapple mixture.

Shape dough into small balls and press onto greased cookie sheet.

Bake at 350 for 8 to 10 minutes. Cool.

Pineapple Icing:

2 1/2 cups powdered sugar   1/2 cup pineapple juice
2 tablespoons soft butter

Stir ingredients together until smoothly blended. If needed, add more powdered sugar for spreading consistency.

Ice cooled cookies.

CUSTARD PIE — House Recipe

5 eggs
1 cup sugar
1 teaspoon vanilla
1/2 cup evaporated milk
2 cups milk
Nutmeg to sprinkle on top

1 9-inch unbaked pie shell

Beat eggs; add sugar and vanilla. Stir in all the milk. Pour into unbaked pie shell. Sprinkle with nutmeg.

Bake at 400 for 10 minutes. Reduce heat to 325 and bake for 25 to 30 minutes longer (until crust is a golden brown and knife inserted in center comes out clean).

OATMEAL PIE — House Recipe

1 cup brown sugar
4 eggs, well-beaten
1/4 cup butter, melted
3/4 cup pancake syrup
1/4 cup evaporated milk
1 teaspoon vanilla
1/2 cup shredded coconut
1/2 cup quick-cooking oatmeal, dry

1 9-inch unbaked pie shell

Mix together brown sugar, eggs and melted butter. Add pancake syrup, milk and vanilla. Stir in coconut and oatmeal. Pour into unbaked pie shell.

Bake at 375 for 10 minutes. Reduce heat to 325 and bake another 35 minutes.

PEANUT BUTTER BARS   House Recipe

1 1/2 cups butter
1 1/2 cups brown sugar
1 1/2 cups white sugar
3 eggs
1 1/4 cups peanut butter
3/4 teaspoon salt

1 1/2 teaspoons soda
1 1/2 teaspoons vanilla
3 cups flour
3 cups oatmeal
1 1/2 to 2 cups
      chocolate chips

Cream together butter and sugars. Beat in eggs and peanut butter. Add remaining ingredients and mix well. Pour batter into a 15 1/2 X 10 1/2 pan. Bake at 350 for 10 to 12 minutes.

Sprinkle with chocolate chips and bake for another 7 minutes.

Topping:

3 cups powdered sugar   1 cup milk
1 1/2 cups peanut butter

Beat together and spread on top of hot bars.

Cool bars before cutting into squares.

LEMON BARS   House Recipe

Crust:

2 cups butter   1/4 cup powdered sugar
4 cups flour

Mix thoroughly together and press into a greased 16 1/2 X 12 1/2" pan.

Bake at 350 for 10 to 12 minutes.

Custard:

8 eggs   1 teaspoon baking powder
4 cups sugar   3/4 cup lemon juice
1/2 cup flour

Beat together until fluffy and pour over top of hot crust. Bake at 350 for 25 minutes or until set.

After removing from oven, sprinkle with powdered sugar.

Cool and cut into squares.

CREAM CHEESE BROWNIES   House Recipe

Step 1   Combine in large mixing bowl:

2 cups flour   2 cups white sugar

Bring to boil and add to dry ingredients:

1 cup water   1/2 cup margarine
1/2 cup shortening   2 tablespoons cocoa

Step 2   Beat together and then add to the batter, beating until smooth:

2 eggs   1/2 cup buttermilk
1 teaspoon soda   1/4 teaspoon salt
1 teaspoon vanilla

Pour batter into 15 1/2 x 10 1/2 pan.

Step 3   Mix the following ingredients together and drop by tablespoons evenly on the batter. Cut through several times with a knife or metal spatula for marbled effect.

1 (8 oz.) package cream   1/2 cup sugar
      cheese   1/2 cup milk chocolate
1 egg, beaten   chips

Sprinkle top with additional chocolate chips and chopped nuts. Bake at 350 for approx. 25 to 30 minutes or until cake springs back when touched lightly in center or wooden pick inserted in center comes out clean.

COOK'S NOTE   This is a very popular item on our dessert bar.

ZUCCHINI BARS — House Recipe

- 3 eggs
- 1 cup brown sugar
- 1 cup white sugar
- 1 cup vegetable oil
- 1 teaspoon salt
- 1 teaspoon baking powder
- 3 teaspoons cinnamon
- 2 teaspoons soda
- 2 cups flour
- 2 cups grated zucchini

Slightly beat eggs; add sugars and oil. Mix well. Sift together dry ingredients. Add dry ingredients alternately with zucchini to egg mixture.

Pour into greased 15 1/2 x 10 1/2 pan. Bake at 350 for 30 minutes. Cool.

Icing:

- 4 oz. cream cheese
- 2 cups powdered sugar
- 1/2 cup soft margarine
- 1 teaspoon vanilla

Mix well together. Spread on cooled bars. Sprinkle with chopped nuts.

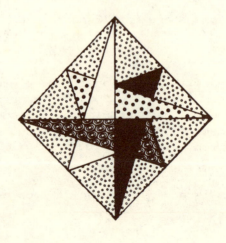

EXCELLENT COATING   Shirley Haarer

1/3 cup Crisco oil   1/3 cup flour
1/3 cup Crisco

Mix all ingredients until well blended. Use to coat casseroles and baking pans for cakes and bread. Store in refrigerator in a tightly covered container. It keeps very well.

FRENCH BREAD   Esther Mishler

Mix together and let cool:

2 cups boiling water   2 tablespoons margarine
2 tablespoons sugar   2 teaspoons salt

Mix together:

2 packages yeast   1/2 cup warm water
1 tablespoon sugar

Combine two mixtures. Then add:

6 to 6 1/2 cups flour

Let stand for 10 minutes; then stir. Let the dough rest again for 10 minutes and stir. Repeat 4 or 5 times. Dough will be like elastic.

Divide dough in halves. Shape each into rectangular loaf of desired length. Make a few diagonal slashes across tops. Let rise 45 minutes. Beat 1 egg; add 2 tablespoons milk; brush over tops of bread before baking. Bake at 400 for 20 minutes.

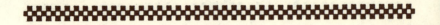

BROWN BREAD   Lucy Mast

Stir together and set aside:

3 tablespoons yeast   1/3 cup very warm water
1 teaspoon sugar

Combine:

1/2 cup cooking oil   2 tablespoons salt
1/2 cup honey   4 cups hot water

While oil-honey mixture is still warm, add yeast and mix.

Stir in 2 or 3 cups at a time:

2 cups whole wheat   10 cups all-purpose flour
    flour

Knead; add more flour if needed until your hands no longer stick to the dough. Let rise in a warm place for 1 1/2 hours. Then punch down, shape and place in 4 loaf pans. Prick tops of loaves with a fork. Brush tops with butter or margarine. Let rise 1 hour.

Bake at 350 for 40 minutes or until done. Butter tops. Turn out of pans to cool.

COOK'S NOTE My Mom's recipe. It is worth going home just to eat her delicious bread!

BRAN DINNER ROLLS   Esther Mishler

3/4 cup whole bran cereal
1/3 cup sugar
1 1/2 teaspoons salt
1/2 cup margarine
1/2 cup boiling water
2 packages dry yeast

2 teaspoons sugar
1/2 cup warm water
1 egg, beaten
3 1/4 to 3 3/4 cups
   unsifted flour

In a large mixing bowl, combine the cereal, 1/3 cup sugar, salt and margarine (cut into pats). Add the boiling water and stir until margarine melts. Set aside to cool to lukewarm.

Add yeast and 2 teaspoons sugar to warm water and stir until dissolved. After the yeast has started to rise a bit, stir into the cereal mixture.

Add beaten egg, then enough flour to make a stiff dough. Turn out on lightly floured board and knead until smooth, 5 - 8 minutes. Place in greased bowl, cover and let rise until double in size (about one hour).

Punch down dough. Divide in half; divide each half into 12 pieces. Shape into rolls and put on greased baking sheet or muffin tins. Let rise 1 hour.

Bake at 375 for 20 to 25 minutes. About 5 minutes before taking from oven, brush tops with margarine to give them a softer crust after they cool.

OVERNIGHT ROLLS   Rebecca Yoder

2 tablespoons yeast   1 1/2 cups buttermilk,
1/2 cup warm water   slightly warmed

Soften yeast in water; stir in buttermilk.

Add:

1 1/2 cups butter, melted   1 teaspoon salt
1 teaspoon soda   4 1/2 cups flour
1/2 cup sugar

Mix and beat about 10 minutes. Dough will be like thick cake dough. Shape and refrigerate 8 hours or overnight. Bake at 375 for 20 to 25 minutes or until golden brown.

BUTTERHORNS   Esther Mishler

1 package dry yeast
1 tablespoon sugar
2 tablespoons very warm
    water
1/2 cup margarine
1 cup cold milk
1/2 cup sugar
1 teaspoon salt
3 eggs, well-beaten
4 cups flour
1/2 cup flour

Mix yeast and 1 tablespoon sugar; stir in very warm water. Let stand. (Be sure to put in large enough bowl, as it will rise fast.)

Melt margarine, then add cold milk, 1/2 cup sugar and salt. Stir in beaten eggs. Add yeast mixture; stir. Add 4 cups flour. (This mixture will be sticky.) Leave in a large covered bowl overnight. (Do not refrigerate.)

The next day, mix 1/2 cup flour into the mixture with a spooon. Divide dough into 4 equal parts. On a floured pastry board, roll out round like a pie crust. Cut into 8 pie-shaped wedges. Roll up from wide end to small end. Place point down on cookie sheet, curving slightly into moon shape. Cover and let rise for 4 hours.

Bake at 375 for 12 minutes or until done.

COOK'S NOTE   I received this recipe from one of our pastors' wives who entertained many guests. This was one you could begin on Saturday evening late, and have fresh baked rolls for dinner and still not have a lot of extra work. Very delicious! And how inviting it smelled when you stepped into her house for Sunday dinner!

RYE BREAD   Barbara Bontrager

1 package dry yeast
1 cup lukewarm water
1 cup milk (scalded & cooled)
1 teaspoon salt
2 tablespoon vegetable oil
2 tablespoons molasses OR brown sugar
2 cups fine rye flour
4 1/2 cups white flour

In large bowl, dissolve the yeast in the water. Add the rest of the ingredients <u>except</u> the white flour. Beat until smooth. Slowly blend in the white flour. Knead 5 to 10 minutes. Let rest 20 minutes. Knead again. Let rise another 20 minutes. Put in a 9 x 5 inch loaf pan and bake at 350 for 40 minutes or un-until a golden brown.

SOFT PRETZELS   Regina Yoder

1 package dry yeast
1/4 cup warm water
2 teaspoons sugar
1/8 teaspoon salt
1 1/4 cups warm water
4 to 5 cups flour
4 teaspoons baking soda
4 cups boiling water
coarse salt

Dissolve yeast in 1/4 cup warm water. Add sugar, salt, and 1 1/4 cups warm water. Beat in flour to make a stiff dough. Knead 10 minutes. Let rise 45 minutes. Punch down and shape into pretzels 1/2 inch thick. Put baking soda and 4 boiling water in a pan; put pretzels 1 or 2 at a time in boiling water for 1 minute or until they float to top. Remove and drain. Put on buttered cookie sheet; sprinkle with coarse salt. Bake at 450 for 12 minutes or until golden brown. Cool on racks.

STRAWBERRY BREAD   Miriam Schrock

1 (10 oz.) package frozen strawberries
4 eggs, beaten
1 1/4 cups oil
3 cups flour
1 teaspoon soda
1 teaspoon salt
3 teaspoons cinnamon
2 cups sugar
1 1/4 cups chopped nuts

Mix together undrained berries, eggs, and oil.

Reserve 1/2 cup flour. Sift rest of dry ingredients into strawberry mixture; stir and blend thoroughly. Stir nuts into reserved flour (this keeps nuts from sinking to the bottom). Stir nuts into the batter.

Pour into two well-greased 9x5x3 inch loaf pans. Bake at 350 for 1 hour. If loaves brown before they are done, put loose tent-shaped foil over them.

FRUIT AND CHEESE BREAD — Barb Bontrager

- 1 cup butter
- 1 (8 oz.) package cream cheese
- 1 1/2 cups sugar
- 4 eggs
- 1 teaspoon vanilla
- 2 1/4 cups flour
- 2 teaspoons baking powder
- 1/2 teaspoon salt
- 1 cup cut-up candied cherries
- 1 cup cut-up candied pineapple
- 1 cup chopped nuts
- 1/4 cup flour (for dredging fruits and nuts)

Cream together butter and cream cheese. Beat in the sugar until fluffy. Add eggs, one at a time, beating well. Add vanilla.

Combine flour, baking powder and salt. Blend into cheese-egg mixture.

Stir fruits and nuts in the 1/4 cup flour to coat. Mix into batter.

Divide batter into 2 greased 9x5x3 inch loaf pans. Bake at 325 for 60 to 70 minutes. Cool in pans on rack for 10 minutes. Remove from pans and cool completely.

MA'S QUICK BANANA BREAD — Barbara Slagel

3 ripe bananas
1 1/4 cups flour
1 cup sugar
1/2 teaspoon salt
1 teaspoon baking soda
2 eggs
1/2 cup oil
chopped nuts (optional)

In a large bowl, mash bananas with a fork. Sift dry ingredients together on wax paper. To bananas, add eggs and oil. Mix well. Add dry ingredients to the banana mixture. Stir only until blended. Dough will be lumpy. Pour into greased and floured loaf pan. Bake at 350 for 75 minutes.

BLUEBERRY TEA BREAD — Barbara Bontrager

3 cups flour
1 1/2 cups sugar
4 1/2 teaspoons baking powder
1/8 teaspoon salt
2 1/4 cups blueberries
3 eggs, slightly beaten
1 1/2 cups milk
4 tablespoon vegetable oil
2 tablespoons orange juice
1 1/2 teaspoons grated orange rind

In large bowl, mix together dry ingredients. Stir in blueberries.

In small bowl, combine the liquid ingredients; mix well. Pour liquid ingredients into the dry ingredients and mix only to moisten. Divide batter evenly between 2 greased 9x5x3 inch loaf pans. Bake at 350 for 55 to 60 minutes or until the loaves are golden brown.

PUMPKIN CHEESE BREAD — Freda LuElla Miller

- 2 1/2 cups sugar
- 1 (8 oz.) package cream cheese
- 1/2 cup margarine
- 4 eggs
- 1 (16 oz.) can pumpkin
- 3 1/2 cups flour
- 2 teaspoons baking soda
- 1 teaspoon salt
- 1 teaspoon cinnamon
- 1/2 teaspoon baking powder
- 1/4 teaspoon ground cloves
- 1 cup chopped nuts

Combine sugar, cheese and margarine; mix at medium speed on electric mixer until well blended. Add the eggs, one at a time, mixing well after each addition. Blend in pumpkin.

Add all dry ingredients mixing just until moistened. Fold in nuts. Pour into 2 greased and floured 9x5x3 inch loaf pans.

Bake at 350 for 1 hour or until wooden pick inserted in center comes out clean. Cool 5 minutes, then remove from pans.

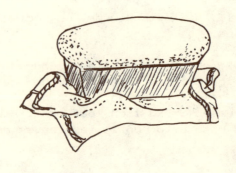

SUPER PANCAKES   Barbara Bontrager

2 eggs, slightly beaten
1/3 cup margarine, softened
1 cup milk
1 1/4 cups flour
4 1/2 teaspoons baking powder
3/4 teaspoon salt
1 teaspoon sugar

Combine eggs and margarine; stir in milk. Add sifted dry ingredients. Beat only until flour is blended. Fry on an oil-coated hot griddle.

Pancake Syrup:
1 cup white sugar
1 cup brown sugar
1 cup light corn syrup
1 cup water
1 teaspoon Maple Flavoring

Mix together and boil 5 minutes.

MUFFINS   Miriam Schrock

1 egg, slightly beaten
1 cup milk
1/4 cup shortening, melted
2 cups flour
3 teaspoons baking powder
1/4 cup sugar
1 teaspoon salt.

Mix egg, milk and shortening in small bowl.

In a larger bowl, combine dry ingredients. Add the liquid ingredients all at once. Stir very gently until all flour is moistened (about 20 strokes). Batter should be lumpy. Do not overmix. Fill greased muffin cups 2/3 full. Bake at 400 for 20 to 25 minutes.

"DIABETIC" RAISIN BRAN MUFFINS — Gladys Miller

1 1/2 cups all bran cereal
1/2 cup boiling water
1 egg, slightly beaten
1 cup buttermilk (skim)
1/4 cup vegetable oil
1/3 to 1/2 cup raisins
1 1/4 teaspoons soda
1/2 cup Sweet & Low
1 1/4 cup flour, sifted

Mix cereal with boiling water stirring to moisten evenly. Set aside to cool.

Add eggs, buttermilk, oil and raisins. Blend well.

Combine dry ingredients; stir into raisin mixture.

Muffins can be baked immediately, or batter can be refrigerated in a tightly covered container for as long as 2 weeks. Bake them as you wish.

After refrigerating, stir batter to evenly distribute raisins before baking.

Spoon batter into cupcake-paper lined muffin tins, filling each 2/3 to 3/4 full. Bake at 350 for about 20 minutes.

ENGLISH MUFFINS IN A LOAF   Mrs. Dan Nissley

2 packages yeast
1/4 cup warm water
6 cups flour
1 tablespoon sugar
2 teaspoons salt

1/4 teaspoon baking soda
2 cups milk
1/2 cup water
cornmeal

Dissolve yeast in 1/4 cup warm water and let it get foamy. Then combine the yeast, 3 cups flour, sugar, salt and soda.

Heat milk and 1/2 cup water until very warm. Stir into flour mixture; beat well. Stir in rest of the flour to make a stiff batter. Spoon into 2 loaf pans that have been greased and sprinkled with cornmeal.

Cover and let rise in a warm place for 45 minutes.

Bake at 400 for 25 minutes. Remove from the pans immediately and cool.

DOUGHNUTS -- I   Sarah Schrock

3 eggs, well-beaten
1 cup sugar
1 cup dairy sour cream
4 cups flour
2 teaspoons baking powder
1/2 teaspoon baking soda
1/2 teaspoon salt
1 1/2 quarts lard, for frying

Mix all ingredients together (except lard). Roll out on flour covered board and cut. (Use lots of flour on rolling pin to prevent sticking!)

Heat lard--it must be very hot. Test by dropping in a small piece of dough; if it floats, the lard is hot enough. Fry the doughnuts a few at a time and drain on towels. Doughnuts can be rolled in granulated or powdered sugar or doughnut glaze. Roll while warm.

DOUGHNUTS -- II   Barbara Bontrager

3 tablespoons butter, softened
1 1/2 cups sugar
2 eggs, well-beaten
3 medium sized potatoes, peeled, boiled & mashed
6 cups flour
1 cup milk
4 teaspoons baking powder
1 teaspoon salt
1 teaspoon cinnamon
1/2 teaspoon nutmeg

Mix all ingredients together. Divide dough into thirds for easier handling. On floured board, roll dough to 1/2 inch thickness and cut. Fry in hot oil until golden brown. Cool, glaze or roll in sugar and cinnamon.

CREAM-FILLED COFFEE CAKE   Mrs. Al Fry

1 1/2 tablespoons yeast
1/2 cup warm water
3/4 cup milk
1/2 cup margarine
1/2 teaspoon salt
1 1/2 teaspoons sugar
2 eggs, beaten

3 1/2 to 4 cups flour

Crumb topping:
1/2 cup brown sugar
1/4 cup flour
1 tablespoon margarine
dash of cinnamon

Dissolve yeast in warm water; set aside.

Heat the milk, melting margarine in it. Add salt and sugar; cool to lukewarm. Add eggs and yeast; mix well and add the flour. Let rise 1 hour.

Divide dough evenly into 4 pie pans or baking pans. Mix ingredients together for the crumb topping and spread over top of dough in pans. Let rise again.

Bake at 400 for 15 minutes. When cakes are cooled, split each cake in half, making 2 layers. Spread filling on bottom layers and put tops back on.

Filling:

4 tablespoons water
1/2 cup white sugar
4 2/3 cups powdered sugar
3/4 cup shortening

2 teaspoons vanilla
1/2 teaspoon salt
2 egg whites, beaten

Boil water and white sugar together for one minute.

Mix powdered sugar, shortening, vanilla and salt together. Blend in sugar-water mixture. Fold in beaten egg whites.

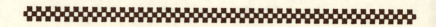

FRUIT SWIRL COFFEE CAKE — Lydia Yoder

4 cups Bisquick baking mix
1/2 cup sugar
1/4 cup butter, melted
1/2 cup milk
1 teaspoon vanilla
1 teaspoon almond extract
3 eggs
1 (21 oz.) can pie filling (apricot, blueberry, or cherry)

Mix all ingredients except pie filling; beat vigorously. about 1/2 minute. Spread 2/3 of the batter (about 2 1/2 cups) in a greased jelly roll pan, or 1/3 of the batter (about 1 1/4 cups) in each of 2 square (9x9) pans.

Spread pie filling evenly over batter (filling may not cover batter completely). Drop remaining batter by tablespoons onto pie filling.

Bake at 350 about 20 to 25 minutes or until light brown. Drizzle with glaze while warm. Serve warm or cooled.

Glaze:
1 cup powdered sugar   1 to 2 tablespoons milk

Blend until smooth and of desired consistency.

CINNAMON FLOP COFFEE CAKE — Ruby Kuhns

2 cups white sugar
4 teaspoons baking powder
2 tablespoons vegetable oil
4 cups flour
2 cups milk

1/4 cup butter, melted
brown sugar
cinnamon
1 cup powdered sugar
milk OR water

Mix well together the white sugar, baking powder and oil. Add flour alternately with milk; mix well. Pour into a greased 13x9 baking pan. Pour the melted butter evenly over the top. Sprinkle with brown sugar and cinnamon. Bake at 350 for about 30 to 35 minutes or until toothpick inserted in center comes out clean. Mix powdered sugar and milk to spreading consistency and drizzle on top.

QUICK MINCEMEAT COFFEE CAKE — Barbara Bontrager

1 3/4 cups flour
3 teaspoons baking powder
1/2 teaspoon salt
1/2 cup sugar, white OR brown
1/2 cup margarine, softened

2/3 cup milk
1 egg, beaten
3/4 cup mincemeat

Topping:
sugar
cinnamon

Combine flour, baking powder and salt. Cut in the shortening. Stir in remaining ingredients and mix well.

Pour into a 9x9x2 baking pan. Sprinkle with sugar and cinnamon. Bake at 375 for 25 to 30 minutes.

CARAMEL PECAN ROLLS — Barbara Bontrager

1 package dry yeast
1 cup warm water
1/4 cup white sugar
1 teaspoon salt
2 tablespoons margarine, softened
1 egg
3 1/4 to 3 1/2 cups all-purpose flour

1/3 cup margarine, melted
1/2 cup brown sugar
1 tablespoon corn syrup
2/3 cup pecan halves

Filling:
2 teaspoons cinnamon
1/2 cup white sugar
softened margarine

In large mixing bowl, dissolve yeast in warm water. Stir in 1/4 cup white sugar, salt, 2 tablespoons margarine, egg and 2 cups flour; beat until smooth. With spoon or hand, work in enough remaining flour until dough is easy to handle. Place in a greased bowl; turn to grease surface. Cover tightly. Refrigerate overnight or up to 5 days.

Combine melted margarine, brown sugar, syrup and pecans. Spread in greased 13x9x2 inch pan.

On floured board, roll dough into a 15 x 9 oblong. Spread with soft margarine and sprinkle with mixed cinnamon and sugar. Roll up, beginning at wide side and seal edge well. Cut into 1 inch slices and put cut side down in prepared pan.

Cover, let rise in warm place until double in size, about 1 1/2 hrs. Bake at 375 for 25 to 30 minutes.

CINNAMON ROLLS   Fern Miller

1 cup milk, scalded   2 eggs
3 tablespoons shortening   3 1/2 cups flour
3 tablespoons sugar   melted butter
1 teaspoon salt   brown sugar
2 packages dry yeast   cinnamon
1/4 cup warm water

Stir shortening, sugar and salt into hot milk. Let set until lukewarm.

Soften yeast in warm water. Add eggs and yeast to lukewarm milk mixture; beat well. Gradually add the flour, stirring briskly. Set in warm place to rise until double in size (about 1 to 1 1/2 hours).

Roll out into rectangle on floured surface. Brush with melted butter, sprinkle with brown sugar and and cinnamon to cover. Roll up lengthwise and cut into 1 inch slices. Put cut side down in greased pan and let rise again for 1 hour. Bake at 400 for 12 to 14 minutes or until golden brown. Glaze with powdered sugar frosting while still warm.

PIE CRUST -- I   Esther Mishler

3 cups flour
1 1/4 cups vegetable
    shortening
1/2 teaspoon salt

1 egg
5 tablespoons water
1 teaspoon vinegar

Mix flour, shortening and salt. Beat egg vigorously and add water and vinegar. Add egg mixture to flour mixture and mix.

When rolling out pie crusts, use the least amount of flour possible. Do not over handle or keep kneading dough. This will make a very flaky crust.

Makes enough dough for 2 9-inch double-crust pies or 4 9-inch single-crust pies.

PIE CRUST -- II   Barbara Bontrager

6 cups pastry flour
2 cups shortening

1 egg
2 tablespoons vinegar

Cut shortening into flour.

Put egg in measuring cup and beat well with fork; fill to 3/4 cup with water and add the vinegar.

Add egg mixture to flour mixture. Mix with hands until well blended, but do not overmix. Roll dough out on flour-sprinkled pastry board.

Recipe makes enough dough for 6 9-inch single-crust pies or 3 9-inch double-crust pies.

PIE CRUST -- III   Susie Ellen Knepp

5 cups pastry flour
4 teaspoons sugar
1/2 teaspoon salt
1/2 teaspoon baking powder
1 1/2 cups lard
2 egg yolks

Put flour in bowl; add sugar, salt, baking powder. Mix in lard until crumbly.

Put egg yolks in measuring cup and add a little water; mix well. Then fill cup with water. Stir egg mixture into flour mixture.

Mix dough until it forms a ball. Roll out on flour sprinkled board.

Makes 3 9-inch double-crusts.

COOK'S NOTE   Pastry flour makes a better crust. New Rinkel is the popular brand used in our community. If using all-purpose flour, decrease flour to approximately 4 1/2 cups.

FRESH FRUIT PIES   Esther Mishler

3/4 cup sugar
1 1/4 cups water
2 tablespoons white Karo
1 (3 oz.) package
     fruit-flavored Jello

5 tablespoons Clear Jel
   OR 2 tablespoons
     cornstarch
fresh fruit
whipped topping

1 9-inch baked pie crust

Combine sugar, water and Karo; bring to boil. Add Clear Jel which has been dissolved in 3 tablespoons water; stir until thickened. Add Jello. Chill.

Prepare fresh fruit while filling is chilling. Wash and drain enough fruit to fill the crust generously. (Dice or slice, if needed.) Carefully stir filling into the fruit. Turn into cooled, baked crust. Refrigerate.

Add whipped topping just before serving.

COOK'S NOTE   Use same flavor Jello as fruit. Good with peaches and strawberries. Blueberries and raspberries are good with blackberry or black raspberry Jello.

RHUBARB PIE DELIGHT — Elsie Kurtz

1 1/2 cups cubed rhubarb
1 cup sugar
4 tablespoons water
1 (3 oz.) box strawberry jello
1 cup liquid whipped topping
1/8 teaspoon salt
1 teaspoon vanilla

CRUST: Combine 2 cups graham cracker crumbs and 1/2 cup butter, melted. Press into a 9-inch pie pan. Chill.

Simmer rhubarb, sugar and water until tender. Add jello; stir until dissolved. Cool until partly set.

Whip the topping, add salt and vanilla. Fold into rhubarb mixture. Pour filling into crust.

Top with additional whipped topping.

CHOCOLATE CHIFFON PIE — Shirley Martin

1 envelope unflavored gelatin
1/2 cup cold water
1 1/2 cups sugar
4 tablespoons cocoa
2 1/2 cups milk
1/8 teaspoon salt
5 cups whipped topping

2 9-inch baked pie crusts

Soften gelatin in cold water. Combine sugar, cocoa, milk and salt; bring to boil. Remove from heat and stir in gelatin. Cool until partially thickened. Fold in whipped topping. Fill baked crusts.

APPLE PIE -- I   Anna Miller

6 apples (or 8, if small)   4 tablespoons Clear Jel
2 cups water   1 teaspoon cinnamon
2 tablespoons butter   1 1/2 cups sugar

1 9-inch unbaked pie shell

Peel apples and slice into bowl.

Bring water and butter to a boil. Mix Clear Jel, cinnamon and sugar together and add enough water to make a paste. Add to the boiling water and stir until thickened. Lower heat and continue cooking 1 to 2 minutes until mixture becomes clear. Stir in apples.

Pour into unbaked pie shell.

Topping:

1/2 cup flour   1 tablespoon butter
1/4 cup brown sugar

Mix flour, sugar and butter together with a fork until crumbly. Sprinkle on top of pie and bake at 400 for 30 minutes or until done.

COOK'S   Adjust amount of sugar, using more or
 NOTE   less depending on tartness of apples.

APPLE PIE -- II   Irene Miller

2 cups apples,   4 tablespoons flour
    chopped fine   4 eggs, well-beaten
3 cups sugar (brown,   10 tablespoons water
    white, or both)   butter & cinnamon

1 9-inch unbaked pie shell

Mix apples, sugar and flour. Stir in beaten eggs and water. Pour into the crust. Put bits of butter and cinnamon on top of filling. Bake at 350 for 30 to 35 minutes or until done.

COOK'S   This apple-custard pie does NOT need
 NOTE   a top crust.

PUMPKIN PIE   Elsie Kurtz

6 eggs   6 teaspoons cinnamon
3 cups white sugar   2 teaspoons salt
3 cups brown sugar   6 cups canned pumpkin
6 tablespoons flour   5 cups milk
1/2 teaspoon ginger   2 cups cream

6 9-inch unbaked pie shells

Beat eggs well. Add sugar, flour, spices and salt. Mix well. Mix in pumpkin. Then stir in milk and cream. Divide evenly into 6 pie shells. Bake at 350 for 50 to 60 minutes or until knife inserted in center comes out clean. Serve chilled.

PUMPKIN CUSTARD PIE   Esther Mishler

1 1/2 cups pumpkin
1 cup brown sugar
1/2 cup white sugar
3 tablespoons flour
1/2 teaspoon cinnamon
1/2 teaspoon nutmeg

1 teaspoon vanilla
1/2 teaspoon lemon juice
5 eggs
2 1/2 cups evaporated milk
2 cups milk
1/2 teaspoon salt

2 9-inch unbaked pie shells

Mix the first eight ingredients together thoroughly. Add eggs to mixture and beat vigorously until thick and creamy. Add evaporated milk and mix in with rubber spatula, then add milk and salt.

Divide evenly into 2 unbaked pie shells. Bake at 400 for 10 minutes, then reduce heat to 375 and bake for 55 minutes.

COOK'S NOTE   If your oven is a higher temperature, you will need to experiment for the last part of the baking time. Pie should not be completely solid before removing from the oven.

CUSTARD PIE   Esther Mishler

2 1/2 cups milk   1/4 teaspoon salt
4 eggs   1 teaspoon vanilla
1/2 cup sugar   nutmeg OR cinnamon

1 9-inch unbaked pie shell

Scald milk. Beat eggs vigorously; add sugar and beat until well blended. Add salt and vanilla. Then stir in scalded milk.

Pour into unbaked pie shell. (Crust will be very full, move carefully to oven to avoid splash-over.) Bake at 400 for 25 to 30 minutes.

COOK'S NOTE Pie is done when filling shakes like jelly; should NOT be solid before removing from oven. It will finish baking while cooling.

OLD FASHIONED SUGAR CREAM PIE   Rebecca Yoder

3 cups sugar (white OR   3 cups evaporated milk
    brown)   4 egg whites
6 tablespoons flour

3 9-inch unbaked pie shells

Mix sugar, flour and milk together. Beat the egg whites until stiff peaks form. Add to sugar-milk mixture. Divide evenly into 3 unbaked pie shells. Bake for 10 minutes at 400; reduce heat to 350 and bake for another 30 to 35 minutes until browned.

RASPBERRY-PEAR PIE   Barbara Bontrager

1/4 cup sugar
2 tablespoons cornstarch
1/2 teaspoon cinnamon
1/2 teaspoon nutmeg
2 tablespoons butter
1 tablespoon lemon juice
1 (10 oz.) package frozen raspberries, thawed & drained, reserve juice
5 cups peeled, sliced pears (Bartlett)

Pastry for 2-crust 9-inch pie

In large saucepan, combine sugar, cornstarch, cinnamon and nutmeg. Stir in 1/2 cup reserved raspberry juice. Cook over medium heat until mixture thickens. Remove from heat; add butter and lemon juice. Stir until butter melts.

Fold in drained raspberries and pears. Turn into bottom crust. Cut decorative slits into top crust for steam to escape and fit top crust over filling.

Brush crust with milk and sprinkle with sugar. Bake at 400 for 40 to 50 minutes or until crust is golden brown. Cool before cutting.

SOUR CREAM LEMON PIE   Mrs. Al Fry

1 cup sugar
3 1/2 tablespoons cornstarch
1 tablespoon grated lemon rind
1/2 cup fresh lemon juice

3 egg yolks, beaten
1 cup milk
1/4 cup butter
1 cup cultured sour cream
whipped cream

1 9-inch baked pie crust

Combine sugar, cornstarch, lemon rind and juice, egg yolks and milk in a heavy saucepan. Cook over medium heat until thickened. Stir in the butter and cool mixture to room temperature.

Stir in sour cream. Pour into baked crust. Cover with whipped cream and garnish with lemon slices. Refrigerate.

LEMON CAKE PIE   Barbara Bontrager

2 eggs, separated
1/8 teaspoon salt
2 tablespoons flour
3/4 cup sugar

grated rind & juice from 1 large OR 2 small lemons
1 cup milk

1 9-inch unbaked pie shell

Beat together the egg yolks, salt, flour and sugar. Add the lemon rind and juice. Stir in the milk.

Beat egg whites until stiff. Fold into egg mixture. Pour into pie shell; bake at 325 for 30 minutes.

CARAMEL CREAM PIE — LorEtta Yoder

3 tablespoons flour
4 eggs, separated
2 tablespoons butter, melted
1 cup brown sugar
1 cup white sugar
1/8 teaspoon salt
3 3/4 cups milk, scalded

2 9-inch unbaked pie shells

Mix flour, egg yolks, butter, sugars, and salt together. Stir in scalded milk. Beat egg whites and fold into the mixture.

Pour into unbaked pie shells. Bake at 400 for 10 minutes; reduce heat to 375 and bake until just golden brown. Don't over bake.

SNOW GHOST PIE — Katie Miller

1/4 cup cocoa
1 cup sugar
1/3 cup cornstarch
1/4 teaspoon salt
3 cups milk
3 tablespoons butter
1 1/2 teaspoons vanilla
whipped cream

1 9-inch baked pie crust

Combine the cocoa, sugar, cornstarch and salt in a saucepan. Gradually stir in milk. Cook until the mixture is thickened, stirring to prevent sticking.

Add butter and vanilla. Pour into baked pie crust.

Top with whipped cream when pie is cool.

PINEAPPLE CREAM PIE   Barbara Bontrager

8 eggs
4 cups sugar
8 tablespoons cornstarch
1 cup cream
1 teaspoon salt

4 teaspoons vanilla
1 (15 oz.) can crushed pineapple
5 cups milk, scalded

4 9-inch unbaked pie shells

Separate 5 eggs. Beat 5 yolks and 3 whole eggs together. Add sugar, cornstarch and cream; mix well. Stir salt, vanilla, and pineapple into egg yolk mixture; then stir in hot milk.

Beat egg whites until stiff and fold into filling. Divide evenly into 4 unbaked shells.

Bake at 450 for 20 minutes. Reduce heat to 375 and bake for 10 to 15 minutes or until golden brown on top and knife inserted in center comes out clean.

VANILLA CRUMB PIE   Shirley Martin

Bottom layer:

3/4 cup brown sugar
1 cup molasses
2 cups water
1 tablespoon flour
1 egg, well-beaten
1 teaspoon vanilla

Top layer:

2 cups flour
1/2 cup brown sugar
1/2 cup margarine
1 teaspoon soda
1 teaspoon cream of tartar

2 9-inch unbaked pie shells

Combine ingredients for bottom layer <u>except</u> vanilla and boil together. Cool. Then stir in the vanilla. Divide filling evenly into pie shells.

Mix the ingredients for top layer into fine crumbs. Spread over filling. Bake at 350 for 45 minutes.

OATMEAL PIE -- I   Elsie Kurtz

2 eggs
1 cup sugar
1 cup syrup (waffle OR clear)

1 cup uncooked oatmeal, one-minute type
1 stick margarine, melted

1 9-inch unbaked pie shell

Beat eggs; add rest of ingredients and mix well. Pour into unbaked pie shell. Bake at 350 for 30 to 35 minutes or until done.

OATMEAL PIE -- II   Sarah Bontrager

4 eggs, well-beaten
1 1/2 cups sugar
2 tablespoons Clear Jel
1/2 cup maple syrup
1 1/2 cups corn syrup
1 cup water

1 1/2 cups quick-cooking oatmeal
1 cup margarine, melted
1 teaspoon salt
1 teaspoon vanilla

2 9-inch OR 3 8-inch unbaked pie shells

Mix together all ingredients. Pour into pie shells. Bake in hot oven (450) until starting to brown. Reduce heat to 400 and bake until done (about 25 minutes).

COOK'S NOTE: For variety, use 1 cup oatmeal and 1/2 cup shredded coconut.

SOUR CREAM RAISIN PIE — Gladys M. Hochstedler

1/2 cup sugar
4 1/2 teaspoons flour
1/8 teaspoon salt
1 teaspoon cinnamon

2 eggs, separated
1 cup sour cream
1 teaspoon lemon juice
1 cup raisins

1 9-inch baked pie crust

Combine the sugar, flour, salt, and cinnamon. Set aside.

Beat egg yolks thoroughly. Blend in dry ingredients. Stir in sour cream, lemon juice and raisins. Cook over low heat until thickened, stirring constantly. Pour into a baked pie shell and cool.

Meringue:

2 egg whites
1/8 teaspoon cream of tartar

4 tablespoons sugar

Beat egg whites and cream of tartar until peaks begin to form. Add the sugar gradually while beating. After sugar is all added, beat until stiff.

Spread on pie. Brown in oven (350) about 12 minutes or until golden brown.

COOK'S NOTE "I made this pie often when I worked for the wife of my husband's uncle from her recipe. It was their favorite and now it is also my favorite."

PUMPKIN GINGERSNAP PIE — Lydia Yoder

1 1/2 cups half & half OR light cream
1 (4-serving size) package Jello vanilla instant pudding and pie mix
3 1/2 cups (8 oz.) Cool Whip, thaw if frozen
1 cup crushed Keebler gingersnap cookies
1/2 cup canned pumpkin
1 1/2 tablespoons pumpkin pie spice
1 cup chopped pecans

1 9-inch graham cracker pie crust

Pour half & half into large bowl. Add pie filling mix and beat with wire whisk until well blended, about 1 minute. Let stand 5 minutes to thicken.

Fold in the whipped topping, gingersnaps, pumpkin, pumpkin pie spice and pecans. Spoon into crust.

Freeze until firm (about 6 hours or overnight). Remove from freezer and let stand about 10 minutes to soften slightly before serving. Return any leftover pie to freezer.

PUMPKIN CHIFFON PIE — Shirley Martin

3 eggs, separated
2/3 cup sugar
1 1/4 cups canned pumpkin
1/2 cup milk
1/2 teaspoon salt
1/2 teaspoon ginger

1/2 teaspoon cinnamon
1/2 teaspoon nutmeg
1 envelope unflavored gelatin
1/4 cup cold water
whipped cream

1 9-inch baked pie crust

Beat the egg yolks. Stir in 1/3 cup sugar, pumpkin, milk, salt and spices. Cook in double boiler until boiling, stirring constantly.

Dissolve gelatin in cold water. Add to hot pumpkin mixture. Chill until slightly thickened.

Beat egg whites until stiff, adding remaining 1/3 cup sugar gradually. Fold beaten egg whites into chilled pumpkin. Pour into baked pie crust.

Chill until firm. Top with whipped cream.

COOK'S NOTE This recipe is one that my mom used every Thanksgiving.

PEACH ICE CREAM PIE — Shirley Martin

- 3 fresh peaches (large)
- 3 tablespoons sugar
- 1 (3 oz.) package lemon gelatin
- 1 pint vanilla ice cream
- 1 cup whipped cream

1 9-inch baked pie crust

Peel, pit and slice peaches thinly. Sweeten with sugar. Let stand 20 minutes.

Drain the peaches. Reserve the juice. Add enough water to make 1 cup.

Bring peach juice to a boil. Mix in lemon gelatin and stir until dissolved. Cut ice cream into pieces and add to the gelatin, stirring until dissolved. Chill until mixture begins to thicken.

Fold peach slices into partially set gelatin mixture. Pour into pie crust and chill several hours or overnight. Garnish with whipped cream.

MINCEMEAT   Sarah Bontrager

4 pounds raisins
20-22 cooking apples,
    peeled & diced
3 quarts sour cherries
1 1/2 quarts strawberries,
    canned or frozen
3/4 quart ground beef,
    browned & drained

1/2 cup vinegar
1 1/2 cups brown sugar
1/2 cup white sugar
2 teaspoons salt
1 1/2 teaspoons pumpkin
    pie spice
1 1/2 teaspoon cinnamon

In a 12 quart pan, boil raisins and apples in about 1 quart water for 5 to 10 minutes.

Add rest of ingredients and boil for about 30 more minutes.

Put in canning jars while boiling hot and seal; then follow manufacturer's directions for canner. Makes approximately 8 quarts.

COOK'S   My mother-in-law's recipe; this has al-
NOTE   ways been our favorite mincemeat recipe.

ANGEL FOOD CAKE — Barbara Bontrager

1 3/4 cups egg whites
1 1/2 teaspoon cream of
    tartar
1/4 teaspoon salt
1 1/3 cups sugar
1 1/4 cups cake flour
1/2 cup sugar

Beat together egg whites, cream of tartar, and salt until soft peaks form. Then beat in 1 1/3 cups sugar a little at a time. Continue beating until stiff. Fold in cake flour and 1/2 cup sugar.

Pour into tube cake pan and bake at 350 for 35 to 40 minutes. Cake should be golden brown on top. Turn pan upside down and let cake cool in pan.

CHOCOLATE SHEET CAKE — Esther Mishler

2 cups sugar
2 cups flour
1 cup water
1/2 cup vegetable
    shortening
1 stick margarine
4 tablespoons cocoa
2 eggs
1/2 cup buttermilk
1 teaspoon soda
1/4 teaspoon salt
1 teaspoon vanilla

Put sugar and flour in large mixing bowl.

Bring water, shortening, margarine and cocoa to full boil. Pour over flour-sugar mixture. Then add eggs, buttermilk, soda, salt and vanilla; mix well.

Pour into 10 X 15 sheet cake pan. Bake at 425 for 15 to 20 minutes.

COWBOY CAKE   Miriam Schrock

2 cups brown sugar
2 cups flour
1/2 cup shortening
1 cup sour milk OR buttermilk
1 teaspoon soda
1 egg
2 teaspoons vanilla
1/2 teaspoon salt

Mix brown sugar, flour and shortening together. Measure out 2/3 cup and set aside.

Mix remainder of sugar-flour mixture with rest of ingredients. Pour into a 9 X 13 inch baking pan. Sprinkle reserved 2/3 cup sugar-flour mixture evenly over the top. (Chopped nuts can be added.)

Bake at 325 for 30 minutes or until done.

CRUMB CAKE   Mrs. Al Fry

1/2 cup margarine
2 cups brown sugar
1/2 teaspoon salt
2 cups flour
1/2 teaspoon soda
1 cup milk
2 eggs
1 cup chocolate chips

Mix together margarine, brown sugar, salt and flour. Set aside 1 cup of these crumbs.

To remaining crumbs, add soda, milk and eggs. Mix well. Pour into a 9 X 13 inch cake pan. Spread chocolate chips evenly on top of batter, then top with the reserved crumbs.

Bake at 350 for 25 to 30 minutes.

RHUBARB CAKE   Dorothy Miller

1 1/2 cups diced rhubarb   1 egg, beaten
1/2 cup sugar   1 cup sour milk
2 cups flour   1 teaspoon soda
1 1/2 cups sugar   1 teaspoon cinnamon
1/2 cup lard   1 teaspoon vanilla

Combine rhubarb with 1/2 cup sugar and set aside.

Mix lard and 1 1/2 cups sugar well together. Stir in egg and milk alternately with dry ingredients; add vanilla and beat well. Add rhubarb mixture and stir until well blended.

Pour batter into a 9 X 13 pan and bake at 350 for about 1 hour or until done.

Topping:

6 tablespoons butter   1/4 cup milk
1 cup shredded coconut   1 cup chopped nuts
2/3 cup brown sugar

Combine all ingredients in a saucepan and cook about three minutes. Pour over cake while still warm.

BANANA TOPSY TURVY CAKE — Barbara Bontrager

1/2 cup butter OR margarine
1 cup sugar
2 eggs
1 teaspoon vanilla
1 1/4 cups flour
3/4 cup buttermilk

1 teaspoon soda
1/2 teaspoon baking powder
1/2 teaspoon salt
1 cup Quaker oats (uncooked)
1/2 cup mashed banana

Topping:

3 tablespoons butter
1/2 cup brown sugar
1/2 cup chopped walnuts

1 (8 oz.) can sliced pineapple, drained

For topping: Melt butter in 9 inch square baking pan. Sprinkle brown sugar over butter; arrange the pineapple slices and sprinkle nuts evenly over the sugar.

For cake: Beat together the butter and sugar until light and fluffy. Blend in eggs and vanilla.

Combine flour, soda, baking powder and salt; add alternately with buttermilk to egg mixture, mixing well after each addition. Stir in oats and banana.

Pour over the "topping." Bake at 350 for 45 to 50 minutes. Loosen sides of cake from pan. Immediately invert on serving plate. Serve warm or cold with whipped cream.

COOK'S NOTE   Topsy Turvy!--the "topping" <u>does</u> go in the bottom of the pan.

GINGERBREAD DELUXE   Esther Mishler

2 cups flour
3/4 teaspoon salt
2 teaspoons baking powder
1/4 teaspoon baking soda
3/4 to 1 teaspoon ginger
3/4 teaspoon cinnamon
1/8 teaspoon cloves
1/2 cup shortening
2/3 cup sugar
2 eggs
2/3 cup light molasses
3/4 cup boiling water

Mix dry ingredients, except sugar, in a small bowl.

In another larger bowl, cream shortening and sugar. Add eggs and beat well. Gradually add molasses as you are beating. Blend dry ingredients into batter. Then add boiling water and blend until smooth.

Pour batter into a well-greased and floured 9 X 13 cake pan. Bake at 350 for 35 to 45 minutes.

FRUIT COCKTAIL CAKE -- I   Marolyn Yoder

2 eggs
1 3/4 cups sugar
1 (17 oz.) can fruit cocktail
1/2 teaspoon salt

1 teaspoon soda
1 teaspoon cinnamon
2 cups flour
brown sugar

Beat together all ingredients except the flour and sugar. Then gradually add flour; mix together 2 to 3 minutes. Pour batter into a greased 9 X 13 cake pan. Sprinkle brown sugar evenly over batter.

Bake at 350 for 30 to 35 minutes. As soon as cake is out of the oven, make the sauce:

2/3 cup evaporated milk
1/2 cup butter

1 cup sugar
1/2 teaspoon cinnamon

Mix ingredients and boil for 3 to 4 minutes until thick, stirring constantly.

Cut cake into serving pieces and pour sauce over the warm cake.

COOK'S NOTE   A friend gave me this recipe. It's fast and easy to make.

FRUIT COCKTAIL CAKE -- II   Anna A. Miller

2 cups flour
1 1/2 cups sugar
1 (17 oz.) can fruit cocktail
1 teaspoon vanilla
1/2 teaspoon salt
2 eggs, well-beaten
2 teaspoons soda
1/2 cup brown sugar
1/2 cup chopped walnuts

Mix together all ingredients except brown sugar and walnuts. Pour batter into a 9 X 13 pan and sprinkle evenly with brown sugar and walnuts. Bake at 325 for 45 minutes.

Icing:
3/4 cup evaporated milk
1 cup shredded coconut
3/4 cup sugar
2 tablespoons margarine

Combine ingredients in pan and cook for 2 minutes; stir to prevent sticking. Pour at once on hot cake.

SALAD DRESSING CAKE   Alma May Kuhns

1 1/2 cups sugar
1 cup salad dressing
3 1/2 tablespoons cocoa
2 cups flour
1 teaspoon soda
1 cup boiling water
1 teaspoon vanilla

Mix together sugar, salad dressing and cocoa; then add flour and soda alternately with hot water. Stir in vanilla. Bake at 325 for 35 minutes.

COOK'S NOTE   Cocoa may be omitted and spices added to suit your taste.

MOM'S APPLE CAKE — Katie Miller

- 2 cups peeled, diced apples
- 1 cup sugar
- 1 egg, well-beaten
- 1 cup sifted flour
- 1 1/2 teaspoons cinnamon
- 1 teaspoon soda
- 1/2 cup chopped nuts, optional

Mix sugar with apples and let stand until sugar is dissolved. Add egg and mix well.

Sift dry ingredients together; stir into apple mixture. Stir in nuts.

Pour into 8 inch square baking pan. Bake at 375 for 40 minutes or until done.

Immediately cover with hot sauce:

- 1/2 cup brown sugar
- 1/2 cup white sugar
- 2 tablespoons flour
- 1 cup water
- 1/4 cup butter OR margarine
- 1 teaspoon vanilla

Combine sugars, flour and water in a saucepan and cook until clear. Stir in butter and vanilla.

COOK'S NOTE It's best to cook the sauce about 15 minutes before the cake is done so it will thicken and cool some before pouring on cake.

TURTLE CAKE   Regina Yoder

1 (18.25 oz.) pkg. German Chocolate Cake Mix
1 (14 oz.) package caramels
1/2 cup margarine
7 oz. sweetened condensed milk
6 oz. chopped pecans
1 cup milk chocolate chips

Prepare cake mix according to package directions.

Pour 1/2 of the batter into a 9 X 13 pan. Bake at 350 for 15 minutes.

Put caramels, margarine and milk in a microwaveable bowl. Melt in the microwave; check and stir every 30 seconds until melted and smooth. Cool slightly and pour over baked cake.

Evenly pour remaining cake batter over the baked layer. Sprinkle with pecans and chips. Bake for 25 minutes more or until done.

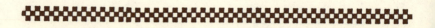

ZUCCHINI CAKE — Lydia Yoder

- 3 cups New Rinkel flour
- 2 cups sugar
- 2 teaspoons baking powder
- 1 teaspoon baking soda
- 1 1/2 teaspoons cinnamon
- 1 teaspoon salt
- 3 cups grated zucchini
- 2/3 cup vegetable oil
- 4 eggs, separated
- 1 cup chopped nuts
- 1 cup raisins, optional

Sift all dry ingredients into a bowl. Make a well in the center. Add zucchini, oil and egg yolks. Mix well, gradually pulling dry ingredients into the liquids. Stir in nuts and raisins.

Beat egg whites until stiff. Fold into cake batter.

Pour into a 9 X 13 cake pan. Bake at 300 for 45 minutes or until done. Frost cooled cake.

Frosting:

- 1/2 cup butter
- 8 oz. cream cheese
- 3 cups powdered sugar
- 1 tablespoon milk

Cream butter and cheese together. Blend in sugar; adding milk if needed for desired consistency.

OATMEAL CAKE
Esther Mishler

1 1/4 cups boiling water
1 cup rolled oats
1/2 cup butter OR margarine
1 cup white sugar
1 cup brown sugar
1 teaspoon vanilla
2 eggs, well-beaten

1 1/3 cups pre-sifted flour
1/2 teaspoon salt
1 teaspoon soda
1 teaspoon baking powder
1 teaspoon cinnamon
1/4 teaspoon nutmeg

Pour boiling water over oats; cover and let stand.

Beat butter and sugars together until creamy. Add vanilla, eggs and oats. Beat in the flour, salt, soda, baking powder, cinnamon and nutmeg.

Bake at 350 for 50 to 55 minutes. Remove from oven and spread frosting on top of cake. Put under the broiler and broil until the frosting is bubbly. CAUTION: This will not take long; watch constantly, do not walk away from the oven.

Frosting:

1/4 cup margarine
1/2 cup brown sugar
3 tablespoons half & half

1/3 cup chopped nuts
3/4 cup flaked coconut

Beat margarine and sugar until creamy. Add half & half; mix well. Stir in nuts and coconut.

COOK'S NOTE A moist cake; raisins may be added, also.

APPLE CAKE   Anna A. Miller

- 1 cup vegetable shortening
- 1 3/4 cup sugar
- 3 eggs, beaten
- 1 teaspoon vanilla
- 2 cups flour
- 1 teaspoon salt
- 1 teaspoon soda
- 1 teaspoon cinnamon
- 2 cups peeled & diced apples
- 1 cup chopped nuts

Cream shortening and sugar and beat in the eggs and vanilla. Sift in dry ingredients. Mix well. Stir in apples and nuts.

Pour into greased 9 x 13 inch cake pan. Cool. Top with with icing:

Icing:

- 1 (3 1/2 oz.) package instant vanilla pudding
- 1 1/2 cups milk.
- 1 (3 1/2 oz.) package dream whip (dry)

Combine ingredients and whip until stiff.

PINEAPPLE UPSIDE DOWN CAKE   Shirley Martin

3 tablespoons margarine
1 cup brown sugar
1 (16 oz.) can sliced
    pineapple
3 tablespoons margarine
1 cup white sugar

3 eggs
1 1/2 cups flour
1/2 teaspoon salt
1 1/2 teaspoons baking
    powder
1/2 cup milk

Melt 3 tablespoons margarine in 8 x 8 baking dish. Mix in the brown sugar. Arrange pineapple slices on top of the sugar mixture.

Cream 3 tablespoons margarine and white sugar. Add eggs one at a time, beating until light. Add flour, salt and baking powder alternately with milk. Pour over the pineapple.

Bake at 350 for 45 to 50 minutes. Invert pan onto serving plate right after removing from oven. Serve while warm. Good with ice cream.

COOK'S NOTE   This dish is one my mom often served and it seemed it never reached around for seconds.

HEAVENLY WHITE CAKE   Gladys M. Hochstedler

2 3/4 cups cake flour
1 1/2 cups sugar
1 teaspoon salt
4 teaspoons baking
     powder
2/3 cup Mazola oil
4 eggs, separated

3/4 cup water
2 teaspoons vanilla
1 teaspoon orange
     extract
1/4 teaspoon cream of
     tartar

Mix and sift together flour, sugar, salt and baking powder. Make a well and add salad oil, egg yolks, water and flavorings. Beat until smooth.

Add cream of tartar to egg whites. Beat until very stiff and peaks form.

Gently fold first mixture into egg whites until well blended.

Bake in an angel food cake pan at 350 for 1 hour.

SPICE CAKE
Miriam Schrock

2 cups brown sugar
1/2 cup shortening,
    mix butter & lard
1 cup sour milk
2 eggs
1/2 teaspoon cloves
1/2 teaspoon allspice
1 teaspoon cinnamon
1 teaspoon soda
2 cups flour

Mix together ingredients in order given. Pour into a 9 X 13 pan. Bake at 350 for 30 to 35 minutes or until done.

PINEAPPLE CAKE
Arlene Miller
Elaine Yoder

2 cups flour
2 cups sugar
2 teaspoons soda
2 eggs
1 (20 oz.) can crushed
    pineapple

Mix all ingredeients together. Pour into a 9 X 13 inch cake pan. Bake at 350 for 35 to 40 minutes.

Arlene's topping:
1 (8 oz.) package
    cream cheese
1/4 cup margarine
1 cup powdered sugar
1 teaspoon vanilla

Cream together cheese and margarine. Blend in the sugar and vanilla. Spread on cooled cake.

Elaine's topping:
1 cup brown sugar
2/3 cup evaporated milk

Boil together for 1 minute and pour over hot cake.

BANANA CAKE   Barbara Bontrager

1 cup shortening   1 teaspoon salt
2 cups sugar   1 1/2 teaspoons soda
4 eggs, beaten   1/2 teaspoon nutmeg
2 teaspoons vanilla   2/3 cup sour milk
4 cups cake flour   2 cups mashed banana

Cream shortening; add sugar gradually. Continue to beat until fluffy. Add beaten eggs and vanilla and beat until light.

Sift flour; measure and sift again with other dry ingredients. Add to shortening mixture, alternately with sour milk. Beat thoroughly after each addition.

Stir in mashed banana until well mixed.

Pour into 9 x 13 inch cake pan. Bake at 350 for 30 minutes or until done.

Cool before frosting.

COOK'S NOTE This is a good, moist cake; and a good way to use up bananas that are getting too ripe to eat.

HOT FUDGE PUDDING CAKE   Barbara Slagel

1 cup flour
2 teaspoons baking powder
1/4 teaspoon salt
3/4 cup white sugar
2 tablespoons cocoa
1/2 cup milk

2 tablespoons vegetable oil
1 cup brown sugar
1/4 cup cocoa
1 3/4 cups hot water

Mix together flour, baking powder, salt, white sugar, 2 tablespoons cocoa, milk and oil. Spread the mixture in a 9 X 13 cake pan.

Mix together brown sugar and 1/4 cup cocoa. Crumble evenly on top of mixture in pan.

Pour hot water over entire surface. <u>DO NOT MIX</u>. The water should settle unevenly over mixture.

Bake at 350 for 45 minutes. Delicous served warm with ice cream.

CHOCO-BUTTERSCOTCH BARS — Leanna Fry

1/2 cup margarine
2 cups brown sugar
3 eggs
2 cups flour
2 teaspoons baking powder
1/8 teaspoon salt
1 teaspoon vanilla
1 cup chocolate chips

Melt margarine; remove from heat and stir in sugar. Blend in eggs. Stir in remaining ingredients.

Spread on baking pan (about 12x16). Bake at 325 for 25 minutes or until done. Do not over bake.

CHOCOLATE CHIP CREAM CHEESE BARS — Mrs. Dan Nissley

1 fudge cake mix
2 eggs
1/3 cup vegetable oil
8 oz. cream cheese
1/3 cup sugar
1 cup chocolate chips

Mix dry cake mix, <u>one</u> egg and oil until crumbly. Reserve 1 cup crumbs. Pat remaining crumbs into ungreased 13 x 9 pan. Bake at 350 for 15 minutes.

Beat cream cheese, sugar and one egg until light and smooth. Stir in chocolate chips. Spread over baked layer. Sprinkle with reserved crumbs. Bake 15 minutes longer. Cool before cutting.

MINCEMEAT-FILLED BARS   Gladys M. Hochstedler

3/4 cup shortening,
   softened (part butter)
1 cup brown sugar
1 3/4 cups sifted flour

1/2 teaspoon soda
1 teaspoon salt
1 1/2 cups rolled oats
1 quart mincemeat

Cream thoroughly shortening and sugar.

Sift together flour, soda and salt. Stir into sugar mixture. Add roll oats; mix thoroughly.

Put 1/2 of the crumb mixture in greased 13 x 9 pan. Press and flatten with hands to cover bottom of pan.

Spread with mincemeat filling. Cover with remaining crumb mixture, patting lightly.

Bake at 400 for 25 to 30 minutes or until lightly browned. While warm, cut into bars and remove from pan.

APPLE BROWNIES — Norma Parrish

2/3 cup butter
2 cups brown sugar
2 eggs
1 teaspoon vanilla
2 cups flour
2 teaspoons baking powder
1/4 teaspoon salt
1 cup chopped apples
1/2 cup chopped nuts
powdered sugar

Cream butter and sugar. Add eggs and vanilla. Mix well. Add dry ingredients; stir well. Stir in the apples and nuts.

Pour into well-greased 13 x 9 pan. Bake at 350 for 30 to 35 minutes. Cool. Sift powdered sugar from flour sifter over top.

COOK'S NOTE "I use more than 1 cup apples. It makes it a little more moist."

LEMON CHEESE BARS — Lydia Yoder

Bottom layer:

1 box yellow cake mix   1/3 cup vegetable oil
1 egg

Mix dry cake mix, egg and oil together until crumbly. Reserve 1 cup crumbs for top layer. Lightly pat remaining crumbs into greased 13 x 9 inch pan. Bake at 350 for 15 minutes.

Top layer:

8 oz. cream cheese   1 cup chopped nuts
1/3 cup sugar   1 cup coconut
1 egg   1 cup reserved crumbs
2 tablespoons lemon juice

Beat together cheese, sugar, egg and juice. Spread over the partially baked layer. Sprinkle with nuts, coconut and reserved crumbs. Bake 15 minutes more.

Glaze:

1 cup powdered sugar   2 tablespoons water
1/4 teaspoon lemon juice

Blend together until smooth. Drizzle over cooled lemon bars.

CHOCOLATE CHIP BROWNIES — Cheryl Hochstetler

2 cups brown sugar
1/2 cup margarine
2 eggs
1/8 teaspoon salt
2 cups flour
1 teaspoon baking powder
1/2 teaspoon soda
1 teaspoon vanilla
1 cup chocolate chips

Beat sugar and margarine together. Beat in eggs. Add dry ingredients and vanilla. Stir in chips. Spread in greased 13 x 9 inch pan.

Bake at 350 for 20 minutes or until done. Cool before cutting.

7 - LAYER BARS — LorEtta Yoder

1/2 cup margarine
2 cups graham cracker crumbs
1 cup coconut
1 cup chocolate chips
1 cup butterscotch chips
1 1/2 cups chopped nuts
1 (14 oz.) can sweetened condensed milk

Melt margarine; mix in cracker crumbs. Press into a 11 x 7 pan. Put coconut, chocolate chips, butterscotch chips and nuts on top. Pour milk over all.

Bake at 350 for 20 to 25 minutes.

APPLE PIE BARS   Mrs. Al Fry

Crust:

2 cups flour
1/2 teaspoon baking powder
1/2 teaspoon sugar
1/2 teaspoon salt
1 cup butter
2 egg, separated

Filling:

4 cups peeled & sliced apples
1/2 cup sugar
1/4 cup flour
1 teaspoon cinnamon
1/4 teaspoon nutmeg

Mix dry ingredients for crust and cut in butter as for pie crust. Stir in the egg yolks until crumbly. Press 1/2 of the crumbs in the bottom of a 15 x 10 jelly roll pan or 13 x 9 cake pan.

Combine filling ingredients. Spread evenly over the crumbs in pan. Sprinkle remaining crumbs evenly on the filling. Spread beaten egg whites over all.

Bake at 350 for 30 minutes if in jelly roll pan or 40 minutes if in cake pan. Cool. Drizzle with powdered sugar glaze if desired.

PUMPKIN BARS   Marlene Miller

2 cups flour
2 teaspoons baking powder
1/2 teaspoon salt
2 teaspoons cinnamon
1 teaspoon soda

2 cups sugar
4 eggs, beaten
2 cups canned pumpkin
1 cup vegetable oil

Combine all ingredients and pour into a greased and floured 15 x 10 baking pan. Bake at 350 for 25 to 30 minutes. Cool.

Icing:

3 oz. cream cheese
6 tablespoons margarine
1 teaspoon milk

1 teaspoon vanilla
2 cups powdered sugar

Cream together cheese and margarine; stir in milk and vanilla until smooth. Blend in powdered sugar. Ice cooled bars.

CREAM CHEESE BARS — Norma Parrish

1/2 cup butter, melted
2 eggs
1 package Dromedary pound cake mix

8 oz. cream cheese
2 eggs
3 1/2 cups powdered sugar
chopped nuts

Bottom layer:

Mix butter, 2 eggs and dry cake mix thoroughly together. Pat into bottom of ungreased 13 x 9 pan.

Top layer:

Soften cream cheese. Whip in 2 eggs and powdered sugar. Spread on top of bottom layer. Cover with nuts.

Bake at 350 for 45 minutes or until set. Sprinkle powdered sugar on top while warm.

BROWNIES — LorEtta Yoder

4 eggs, beaten
2 cups sugar
1 1/2 cups flour
1 cup vegetable oil

1 teaspoon salt
2 teaspoon vanilla
2 1/2 tablespoons cocoa
1/2 cup chopped nuts

Combine all ingredients in order and pour into a greased 13 x 9 pan. Bake at 375 for 20 minutes or until done. Sprinkle powdered sugar on top while still warm. Cool before cutting into squares.

PEPPERNUTS   Greg Beachey

3 cups sugar
1 1/2 cups margarine
3 eggs
1 cup sour cream
1 1/2 teaspoons soda
1 cup brown sugar
1 teaspoon salt

1 teaspoon each: allspice
   cardamom   mace
   anise   nutmeg
   cloves   ginger
10 cups (or more) flour
1 1/2 teaspoons baking powder

In a very large bowl, combine all the ingredients <u>except</u> flour and baking powder. Sift flour and baking powder into mixture one cup at a time. Continue mixing (your hands will work best) until you have a stiff dough.

Roll dough into rolls about the diameter of a nickel. Refrigerate overnight. Slice 1/4 to 1/2 inch thick. Bake at 350 for 10 to 15 minutes or until brown.

COOK'S NOTE   Peppernuts (Pfeffernusse) are a very old traditional Swiss-German holiday cookie. Many variations exist, but this is what I believe is close to the original. (It's been in our family for years and years.) Be careful, these can be habit forming!

CHRISTMAS COOKIES
Esther Mishler

- 3 eggs
- 1 cup sugar
- 1 cup margarine, softened
- 1 teaspoon soda
- 2 teaspoons cream of tartar
- 1/2 teaspoon vanilla
- 4 cups flour

Beat eggs for 5 minutes until thick and yellow. Add sugar gradually, beating until thick and creamy. Add margarine and beat until thoroughly blended. Blend in soda, cream of tartar and vanilla. Add 2 cups flour and mix. Add 1 cup flour twice more and mix with wooden spoon. (Less flour may be needed, depending on brand.) Roll out adding as little flour as necessary to cut out. Gently lift cut out cookies onto cookie sheets. Bake at 350 no longer than 6 to 8 minutes. Cookies should look pale, <u>not</u> brown.

Cream Cheese Frosting:

- 3 oz. cream cheese
- 1/4 cup margarine
- 3 cups powdered sugar
- 2 tablespoons milk
- 1/2 teaspoon vanilla

Use electric mixer or pastry blender to mix softened cream cheese and margarine into powdered sugar. Add milk and vanilla and beat until smooth. Spread on Christmas cookies or any sugar cookie.

COOK'S NOTE For Christmas cookies, divide frosting in small portions and add a few drops of food color for a colorful plate of cookies.

Store frosting in refrigerator. Bring to room temperature, stir vigorously. It can be used until the last drop.

ANDY'S COOKIES   Sarah Schrock

1/4 cup butter
1/2 cup lard
2 cups brown sugar
1/2 cup white sugar
3 eggs
4 1/2 cups flour
3 teaspoons baking powder
1 teaspoon salt
1/3 cup evaporated milk
2/3 cup whole milk
1 teaspoon soda
Optional flavoring:
1 teaspoon vanilla
1/2 teaspoon nutmeg
1/2 teaspoon lemon flavor

Thoroughly cream both kinds of shortening and sugar. Beat in eggs until light and fluffy.

Sift flour, baking powder and salt together. Add to sugar mixture alternately with milk to which the soda has been added.

Drop by teaspoon on cookie sheet. Bake at 375 for 8 to 10 minutes or until golden brown.

MOM'S OATMEAL COOKIES — Fannie Yoder

1 1/2 cups brown sugar
3/4 cup shortening
6 tablespoons sour milk
2 eggs, beaten
3/4 teaspoon vanilla
1 1/2 cups sifted flour
3/4 teaspoon soda
1/2 teapoon salt
3 cups oatmeal
raisins or nuts

Mix thoroughly in order given, stirring in raisins and nuts last. Shape in balls and flatten with a wet fork. Bake on greased cookie sheet at 375 for 8 to 10 minutes.

CHOCOLATE CHIP OATMEAL COOKIES — Mrs. James L. (Barbara) Miller

3/4 cup butter
1/2 cup brown sugar
1/2 cup white sugar
2 eggs
1 cup plus
  2 tablespoons flour
1 teaspoon baking powder
1/4 teaspoon salt
1/3 cup milk
1 teaspoon vanilla
3 cups oatmeal
1/2 cup chopped nuts
6 oz. chocolate chips

Cream shortening and sugars thoroughly. Beat in the eggs, one at a time. Sift flour, baking powder and salt; add to creamed mixture alternately with milk. Stir in vanilla, then oatmeal, nuts and chips.

Drop by teaspoon on greased cookie sheet. Bake at 375 for 12 minutes.

FAVORITE CHOCOLATE CHIP COOKIES   Fern Miller

1 cup brown sugar
1 cup white sugar
1 1/2 cups butter, softened
2 eggs
1 teaspoon vanilla

3 cups flour
1 1/2 teaspoons soda
1 teaspoon salt
3 cups chocolate chips
2 cups chopped pecans

In large bowl combine, sugars and butter; beat until creamy about 3 to 5 minutes. Beat in eggs and vanilla.

Combine flour, soda and salt; gradually blend into the sugar mixture. Stir in the chocolate chips and nuts. Drop by rounded teaspoons onto ungreased baking sheet. Bake at 375 for 8 to 10 minutes.

SUGAR COOKIES   Susie Ellen Knepp

2 cups white sugar
2 cups brown sugar
2 cups lard or shortening
4 eggs

2 cups milk
2 teaspoons soda
4 teaspoons baking powder
1 teaspoon vanilla
8 cups flour

Cream lard and sugars together thoroughly. Add one egg at a time, beating well after each. Stir in milk, soda, baking powder and vanilla. Add flour and mix well. Drop by teaspoonful on cookie sheet. Bake at 300 for 8 to 10 minutes or until done.

PUMPKIN COOKIES   Kim Ray Mishler

1 1/4 cups margarine
3 cups sugar
2 eggs, beaten
1 (16 oz.) can pumpkin
12 oz. chocolate chips
   OR 6 oz. chocolate &
   6 oz. butterscotch
1 cup chopped nuts

6 cups sifted flour
3 teaspoons cinnamon
1 1/4 teaspoon pumpkin
   pie spice
3 teaspoons soda
1 1/4 teaspoon cream of
   tartar

Cream margarine and sugar. Stir in eggs, pumpkin, chips and nuts. Mix well.

In a separate bowl, combine dry ingredients. Gradually stir dry ingredients into pumpkin mixture; mix well.

Drop by teaspoon on greased cookie sheet. Bake at 350 for 12 to 15 minutes. Don't overbake.

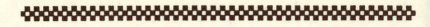

COCONUT OATMEAL COOKIES   Gladys M. Hochstedler

1 1/2 cups sifted flour
1 teaspoon soda
1 teaspoon salt
1 cup butter
1 cup brown sugar
1 cup white sugar
2 eggs
3 cups oatmeal (quick)
1/2 cup chopped pecans
   OR black walnuts
1 1/2 cups flaked coconut

Sift together flour, soda and salt. Cream butter and sugar together; mix until light and fluffy. Add eggs, flour mixture, oatmeal, nuts and coconut; mix thoroughly after each additon.

Divide dough into thirds. Shape each into a roll 2 inches in diameter. Wrap in waxed paper; chill until firm.

Bring cookie rolls to room temperature (about 1/2 hr. or until soft enough to dent when pressed with finger). Cut in 1/8 inch slices. Bake on ungreased cookie sheet at 375 for 10 minutes.

WORLD'S BEST SUGAR COOKIES — Sarah Bontrager

1 cup butter
1 cup powdered sugar
1 cup white sugar
1 cup vegetable oil
2 teaspoons vanilla
2 eggs
5 cups flour
1 teaspoon salt
1 teaspoon soda
1 teaspoon cream of tartar

Cream the butter and sugars until light and fluffy. Blend in oil and vanilla. Beat in eggs. Sift dry ingredients together and stir into sugar mixture.

Shape into balls; put on an ungreased cookie sheet and press with a glass dipped in sugar. Bake at 350 for 15 to 20 minutes.

ZUCCHINI DROP COOKIES — Katie Miller

1/2 cup butter or Crisco
1 cup white sugar
1 egg
1 cup zucchini, peeled and grated
1 teaspoon soda
2 cups flour
1/2 teaspoon salt
1/2 teaspoon nutmeg
1 teaspoon cinnamon
1/2 teaspoon cloves
1/2 cup raisins

Beat shortening, sugar and egg together; beat in zucchini and soda. Stir in flour, salt and spices. Mix in raisins. Drop from teaspoon on cookie sheet.

Bake at 375 for 15 minutes or until done. Frost or eat plain.

SQUASH OR PUMPKIN COOKIES — Anna A. Miller

- 2 cups shortening
- 2 cups white sugar
- 2 eggs
- 1 (16 oz.) can pumpkin OR 2 cups squash
- 2 teaspoons vanilla
- 4 cups sifted flour
- 2 teaspoons baking powder
- 1 teaspoon baking soda
- 1 teaspoon salt
- 2 teaspoons cinnamon
- 1 teaspoon nutmeg
- 1 teaspoon allspice
- 1 cup chopped nuts OR dates OR raisins

Cream together shortening and sugar. Beat in eggs and squash or pumpkin. Add the remaining ingredients and mix well. Drop by teaspoon on cookie sheet and bake at 350 for 15 minutes. Frost when still warm or leave plain.

GINGER COOKIES — Esther Mishler

- 3/4 cup shortening
- 1 cup brown sugar
- 1 egg
- 1/4 cup mild molasses
- 2 1/4 cups flour
- 2 teaspoons soda
- 1/4 teaspoon salt
- 1/2 teaspoon cloves
- 1 teaspoon cinnamon
- 1 teaspoon ginger

Cream shortening and sugar; add egg and beat well. Add molasses, soda, salt and spices and mix. Stir in flour. Chill dough.

Roll in small balls the size of a walnut. Dip in granulated sugar. <u>Do not press down.</u> Sprinkle with water and bake at 375 for 10 to 12 minutes. Do not overbake. Let cookies cool on cookie sheet a minute or two before removing.

MONSTER COOKIES — Esther Mishler

6 eggs
2 cups brown sugar
2 cups white sugar
1 1/2 teaspoons vanilla
1 1/2 teaspoons corn syrup
1 cup margarine, softened
4 teaspoons soda
3 cups peanut butter, smooth or crunchy
9 cups oatmeal
1 cup chocolate chips
8 ounces M & M's

Mix eggs and sugars together, beat well. Blend in vanilla, corn syrup, soda, margarine, and peanut butter. Then add oatmeal and cup chocolate chips. Mix well.

Drop on cookie sheet and spread slightly. Then add 2 eyes and a nose made of M & M's to make cookies look like monsters.

Bake at 375 for 10 to 12 minutes.

COOK'S NOTE The recipe can easily be cut in half if you prefer a smaller quantity.

Recipe is a favorite of my children growing up and now my grandchildren.

You may think I left out the flour but I didn't. The recipe contains no flour. Cookies are a bit pliable when you first take them out of the oven. Let set for about 1 or 2 minutes before removing them from the cookie sheet.

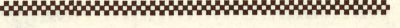

PUFF COOKIES — Miriam Schrock

- 1 cup shortening
- 1 cup brown sugar
- 2 eggs
- 2 3/4 cups flour
- 1 teaspoon cream of tartar
- 1 teaspoon baking powder
- 1 teaspoon soda
- 1/2 teaspoon salt
- 2 tablespoons sugar
- 2 teaspoons cinnamon
- chocolate chips, optional

Mix shortening, sugar and eggs thoroughly.

Sift together dry ingredients except white sugar and cinnamon; blend into egg mixture. Chill.

Form into balls and roll in mixture of sugar and cinnamon. (You may need more sugar and cinnamon.) Place 2 inches apart on ungreased cookie sheet. Top with a few chocolate chips if desired.

Bake at 375 for 8 to 10 minutes.

SWEDISH CREAM WAFERS Barb Bontrager

1 cup butter, softened
2 cups flour
1/3 cup whipping cream
Granulated sugar

Mix thoroughly butter, flour and cream. Cover and chill.

Work with about 1/3 of the dough at a time; keep remaining dough chilled.

Roll dough out 1/8 inch thick on floured board. Cut into 1 1/2 inch rounds. Transfer rounds with spatula to waxed paper heavily covered with granulated sugar; turn each round so that both sides are coated with sugar.

Put on ungreased baking sheet. Prick each wafer about four times with a fork.

Bake at 375 for 7 to 9 minutes or just until set, but not brown. Cool.

Put cookies together in pairs with creamy filling.

Creamy filling:

1/4 cup butter, softened
1 teaspoon vanilla
3/4 cup powdered sugar

Cream butter, sugar and vanilla together until smooth and fluffy. Add few drops of water if too stiff to spread. Tint with a few drops of food color.

COOK'S NOTE I like to sprinkle red and green sugar on the wafers at Christmas time.

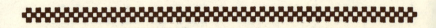

WHOOPIE PIES

Joan Weaver
Marilou Miller

1 cup shortening
2 cups white sugar
2 eggs, beaten
4 cups sifted flour
1/2 cup cocoa

2 teaspoons soda
2 teaspoons salt
1 cup sour milk
2 teaspoons vanilla

Cream sugar and shortening together. Beat in the eggs. Add dry ingredients alternately with the sour milk and vanilla; mix well after each addition.

Drop by teaspoonfuls on cookie sheets. Bake at 375 for 10 to 12 minutes.

When cooled, put 2 cookies together sandwich-style with filling between.

Joan suggests:

1/2 cup vegetable shortening
1 1/2 teaspoons vanilla

5 tablespoons flour
5 tablespoons milk
3 cups powdered sugar

Marilou suggests:

2 egg whites, beat stiff
4 tablespoons flour
1/2 cup Crisco

2 teaspoons vanilla
4 tablespoons milk
2 cups powdered sugar

Blend all ingredients together until very smooth and well blended. (May need more sugar.)

BUTTERSCOTCH OATMEAL COOKIES — Ruby Kuhns

- 1 cup shortening
- 1 cup white sugar
- 1 cup brown sugar
- 2 eggs
- 1 teaspoon vanilla
- 2 cups flour
- 1/2 teaspoon baking powder
- 1/2 teaspoon salt
- 1 teaspoon baking soda
- 2 cups oatmeal
- 1 cup flaked coconut
- 1 cup butterscotch chips

Cream shortening and sugars. Beat in eggs; stir in vanilla.

Sift in dry ingredients and mix well. Stir in oatmeal, coconut and butterscotch chips.

Shape into small balls. Press lightly onto cookie sheet.

Bake at 350 about 15 minutes or until done. Don't overbake.

DATE PUDDING   Barbara Bontrager

1 1/4 cups chopped dates   1 teaspoon soda
1 1/4 cups boiling water   1 tablespoon butter

Mix together and let stand until cold. Then add:

1 cup sugar   1 teaspoon vanilla
2 cups flour   1/2 cup chopped pecans
1 egg   OR walnuts

Mix well and pour into 9x13 cake pan. Bake at 400 for 25 to 30 minutes. Cool.

Cut into 1 inch squares. Layer cake squares and whipped topping in a bowl; ending with topping.

Option: Add sliced bananas with the whipped topping. Garnish with cherries. An attractive dish!

COOK'S NOTE   This was my grandma's recipe. It is best when layered just before serving to keep topping from making the cake soggy.

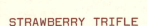

STRAWBERRY TRIFLE   Shirley Martin

white cake mix   2 tablespoons butter
2/3 cup sugar   2 teaspoons vanilla
1/4 teaspoon salt   1 cup whipping cream,
2 tablespoons cornstarch   whipped
1 1/2 cups milk   1 quart strawberries
3 egg yolks, beaten   1/2 cup sugar

Bake cake in a jelly roll pan according to package directions. After cake has cooled 10 minutes, remove from pan. Split in half lengthwise. Set aside.

Mix together 2/3 cup sugar, salt and cornstarch. Stir in milk. Cook until boiling. Gradually add a little hot milk to beaten eggs, then blend all of the egg mixture into milk, stirring well. Cook until thickened. Remove from heat, add vanilla and butter. When cool, add whipped cream.

Crush berries and stir in 1/2 cup sugar. Divide in half.

To assemble: In 3 quart serving bowl, put 1 layer of cake. Over the cake layer spread 1/2 berries. Top with another layer of cake. Spread pudding over this layer. Top with another layer of cake. Spread with remaining berries. Top with cake layer.

Dessert may reach higher than rim of dish. Refrigerate 4 to 5 hours before serving. When ready to serve sprinkle with powdered sugar. Garnish edges of dish with dallops of whipped cream.

FRUIT PIZZA -- I   Esther Bontrager

Dough:

1/2 cup butter	1 1/2 cups flour
3/4 cup sugar	1 teaspoon baking powder
1 egg	1/4 teaspoon salt

Mix butter, sugar and egg together. Stir in the dry ingredients. Chill 1 hour. Line 14 inch pizza pan with dough. Bake at 375 for 12 minutes or until light brown. Cool.

Filling:

8 oz. cream cheese, softened	1/2 cup orange marmalade
1/2 cup sugar	1 teaspoon water
1/2 teaspoon vanilla	assorted well-drained canned or fresh fruit

Blend cheese, sugar and vanilla together and spread evenly over crust.

Arrange fruit attractively over cheese filling. Mix marmalade and water; heat just until the marmalade melts. Glaze fruit.

COOK'S NOTE — Suggested fruit: seedless grapes, pineapple, strawberries, blueberries, kiwi, peaches, bananas.

FRUIT PIZZA -- II

Lydia Yoder

1/2 cup butter
1/2 cup brown sugar
1 egg
1 1/3 cups flour
1 teaspoon baking powder
1/8 teaspoon salt
8 oz. cream cheese
3/4 cup powdered sugar
1 teaspoon milk
1 teaspoon vanilla
2 cups pineapple juice
  (OR other fruit juice)
1/2 cup white sugar
4 teaspoons Clear Jel

Cream together butter and brown sugar; beat in egg. Stir in flour, baking powder and salt. Spread dough on a greased pizza pan or cookie sheet. Bake at 375 for 10 minutes or until light brown. Cool.

Cream together cheese and powdered sugar; blend in milk and vanilla. Spread over baked crust.

Mix fruit juice, white sugar and Clear Jel; cook until thickened. Spread over cheese filling.

CAKE DESSERT

Ruby Kuhns
Leanna Fry

1 (18 oz.) box white cake mix
1 (8 oz.) package cream cheese
1 cup powdered sugar
1 cup whipped topping
1 can pie filling (about 2 cups)

Bake cake as directed on package in 9x13 inch pan. Cool.

Blend together cheese and sugar. Add whipped topping to cheese mixture and spread on top of cake. Spoon pie filling evenly over all.

COOK'S NOTE Recipe is good with apple, blueberry, cherry or pineapple filling.

BLUEBERRY CHEESE CAKE

Kaylene Miller

16 graham crackers
3/4 cup sugar
1/4 cup butter, melted
2 (8 oz. size) packages cream cheese
1 cup sugar
2 eggs, well-beaten
1 teaspoon vanilla
1 can blueberry pie filling (about 2 cups)
whipped cream

Crush crackers and mix in 3/4 cup sugar and butter. Press into 9x13 baking dish. Blend together cheese and 1 cup sugar and mix in eggs and vanilla. Spread over crust. Bake at 375 for 15 minutes. Cool. Spoon pie filling over top; chill. Top with whipped cream.

APPLE DESSERT — Esther Mishler

3 cups peeled & diced apples
1 1/2 cups sugar
2 eggs, beaten
1 1/2 cups flour
2 1/4 teaspoons cinnamon
1 1/2 teaspoon soda

whipped topping

Stir apples and 1 1/2 cups sugar together. Mix in eggs, flour, cinnamon and soda. Bake in a 9 x 13 baking dish at 350 for 35 minutes. Let cool slightly. Then pour <u>cooled</u> prepared syrup over the top. Cool and top with whipped topping.

Syrup:

3/4 cup brown sugar
1/2 cup white sugar
3 tablespoons flour
1 1/2 cups water
1/4 cup margarine
1 1/2 teaspoons vanilla

Mix sugars and flour together; then add water and cook until thick. Blend in margarine and vanilla. Cool before pouring over cake.

COOK'S NOTE — This can be varied by cutting cake into pieces; layer cut cake, syrup and whipped topping in a glass dish. Very attractive and almost tastes like date pudding but not as rich.

CROW NEST PUDDING   Elaine Yoder

1 1/2 cups flour
1 cup sugar
1 1/2 teaspoons baking
    powder
1/8 teaspoon salt

1 tablespoon butter
1 egg, slightly beaten
1/2 cup milk
1 teaspoon vanilla

Measure dry ingredients into a bowl. Mix in remaining ingredients. Makes a stiff batter. Pour into 8x8 inch pan. Bake at 375 for 20-30 minutes. When cool, cut into squares. Serve with warm sauce.

Sauce:
1/2 cup sugar
2 tablespoons cornstarch

2 cups milk
1 teaspoon vanilla

Mix sugar and cornstarch. Stir in milk and bring to a boil, stirring constantly; add vanilla. Pour over cake squares and serve while sauce is warm.

COOK'S NOTE   This is my grandmother's recipe. Can be eaten with fruit and milk. Our family's favorite is frozen blueberries.

PUMPKIN CAKE ROLL — Katie Miller

Cake:

3 eggs
1 cup white sugar
2/3 cup canned pumpkin
1 teaspoon lemon juice
3/4 cup flour
1 teaspoon baking powder
2 teaspoons cinnamon
1 teaspoon ginger
1/2 teaspoon nutmeg
1/2 teaspoon salt

Beat eggs at high speed for 5 minutes. Beat in the white sugar until well blended. Stir in pumpkin and lemon juice.

Combine flour, baking powder, spices and salt; fold into pumpkin mixture. Spread in greased and floured 15x10 jelly roll pan. Bake at 375 for 15 minutes.

Turn cake out on a linen towel heavily dusted with dusted powdered sugar. Starting at wide end, roll towel and cake together. Cool.

Filling:

1 cup powdered sugar
2 (3 oz. size) packages cream cheese
4 tablespoons butter
1/2 teaspoon vanilla

Mix all ingredients together until smooth. Unroll cooled cake. Spread with filling to within 1 inch of edges. Roll up and chill. Dust with powdered sugar just before serving.

ICE CREAM ROLL   Esther Mishler

5 eggs, separated
2 tablespoons water
3/4 cup sugar
6 tablespoons cake flour
1 teaspoon baking powder

6 tablespoons cocoa
1/2 teaspoon salt
powdered sugar
1/2 gallon ice cream, any favorite flavor

Combine 5 egg yolks and 2 tablespoons water. (Eggs beat best at room temperature.) Beat yolks at least 5 minutes. Gradually add sugar and beat well.

Sift dry ingredients together and gently fold into yolk mixture with rubber spatula. Set aside.

Beat egg whites until stiff. Fold the two mixtures together with rubber spatula.

Line sheet cake pan with waxed paper. Spread batter in paper lined pan. Bake at 350 for 25 minutes.

Slightly dampen a tea towel and spread on counter top. Cover with a sheet of waxed paper and sprinkle with powdered sugar. Turn baked cake upside down on powdered sugar. Remove and discard waxed paper from bottom of cake. Quickly roll cake <u>and</u> waxed paper in jelly roll fashion; then roll into towel. Cool.

Carefully unwrap cooled cake. Open all sides of ice cream carton. Cut the ice cream into 1/2 inch thick slices and arrange to cover whole cake. Then quickly roll up cake. Use knife to smooth ends of cake. Wrap cake roll tightly in aluminum foil and freeze.

COOK'S NOTE   ONLY 6 tablespoons of flour! A tradition at Christmas for our family. Nice all year long when entertaining in the evening.

APPLE CINNAMON PUFFS   Ruby Kuhns

6 to 8 apples
1 cup sugar
1 cup water
red food color
1 1/2 cups flour
2 teaspoons baking powder
1/2 teaspoon salt
1/4 cup shortening
3/4 cup milk
2 tablespoons butter
2 tablespoons sugar
1/2 teaspoon cinnamon

Peel and slice apples. Put in a 9 x 12 baking dish. Boil to a syrup: 1 cup sugar, water and food color. Pour syrup over apples.

Sift together flour, baking powder and salt; cut in shortening with a pastry blender. Stir in the milk. Spread on top of apples.

Mix butter, sugar and cinnamon together till crumbly. Sprinkle over top.

Bake at 450 for 30 minutes or until the apples are tender.

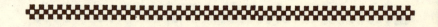

APPLE CRISP -- I   Carolyn Miller

5 to 6 apples
1 cup flour
1/2 cup sugar
1 teaspoon baking powder
3/4 teaspoon salt
1 egg
1/2 margarine, melted
1/2 teaspoon cinnamon

Slice apples into bottom of 9x9 greased baking pan. Sift flour, sugar, baking powder and salt together. Add egg and mix well until crumbly; sprinkle evenly over apples. Pour margarine over top. Sprinkle with cinnamon.

Bake at 350 for 30 to 40 minutes.

APPLE CRISP -- II   Miriam Schrock

1 quart peeled & sliced apples
1/2 cup water
1 cup flour
3/4 cup brown sugar
3/4 cup white sugar
5 tablespoons butter

Put apples in a buttered baking dish; pour water over them. Mix other ingredients until crumbly. Sprinkle over the apples. Bake at 350 for about 45 minutes.

Serve with ice cream or whipped cream.

BUTTER BRICKLE & PEACH DESSERT — Shirley Haarer

1 (29 oz.) can sliced peaches
1 (18 oz.) Butter Brickle cake mix
1/2 cup margarine, melted

Put peaches and juice in a 9x13 inch baking dish. Sprinkle dry cake mix evenly over peaches. Drizzle margarine over cake mix. Bake at 350 for 35 to 40 minutes or until done. Can be served with ice cream or whipped topping.

CINNAMON PUDDING — Becky Kuhns

2 cups brown sugar
1 1/2 cups water
2 tablespoons butter
1 cup sugar
2 cups flour
2 teaspoons baking powder
1 teaspoon cinnamon
2 tablespoons soft butter
1 cup milk
1 cup chopped pecans

Combine brown sugar, water and 2 tablespoons butter and boil. Pour into an 8x8x2 inch baking dish. Sift together flour, sugar, baking powder and cinnamon. Beat in softened butter and milk. Pour over brown sugar mixture in pan. Sprinkle pecans evenly over the batter. Bake at 350 for 45 minutes or until done. Serve with whipped topping.

COOK'S NOTE: We also sometimes pour the syrup over the batter. Some think it's better that way.

BREAD PUDDING -- I   Regina Yoder

2 cups milk
4 cups coarse bread
    crumbs
1/4 cup butter, melted
1/2 cup white sugar
1/2 cup brown sugar

1 cup raisins
2 eggs, slightly beaten
1/4 teaspoon salt
1/2 teaspoon cinnamon
1/2 teaspoon nutmeg

Heat milk to scalding and pour over bread crumbs. Add remaining ingredients; mixing well. Pour into a buttered, 1 1/2 quart casserole. Bake at 350 for 40 to 45 minutes. Serve warm.

BREAD PUDDING -- II   Cheryl Hochstetler

5 cups milk
8 eggs
bread, torn or cubed

1 1/2 cups sugar
2 teaspoons vanilla

Loosely fill a buttered 9x13 baking dish with torn or cubed bread. Heat milk to scalding. Beat eggs; then beat in sugar and vanilla. Stir the hot milk into the eggs, gradually adding a small amount of milk at a time to avoid cooking the eggs. Pour over bread. Bake at 350 for 35 to 40 minutes. Cool slightly and pour on prepared syrup.

Syrup: 3 cups brown sugar   6 cups water
       2 cups white sugar   3/4 cup margarine
       3/4 cup flour   2 tablespoons vanilla

Mix sugars, flour and water and boil until thickened. Stir in margarine and vanilla.

PEACH CRISP GOOD DESSERT   Gladys M. Hochstedler

1/2 cup wheat germ
1/2 cup unsifted flour
1/2 cup brown sugar
1/2 teaspoon nutmeg
1/2 teaspoon cinnamon
1/3 cup butter
frozen sliced peaches, thawed
2 tablespoons cornstarch
2 tablespoons lemon juice

Mix together dry ingredients. Cut in butter with a pastry blender until the mixture looks like fine crumbs. Set aside.

Drain peaches, reserve juice. Combine peach syrup, cornstarch and lemon juice in saucepan. Cook until thickened stirring constantly. Add peaches. Heat. Pour into shallow baking pan. Sprinkle with wheat germ mixture.

Bake at 375 for 20 to 25 minutes until topping is crisp and brown and syrup bubbles appear around edges. Serve plain or topped with whipped cream or ice cream.

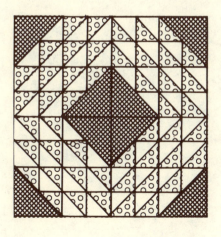

NOTES

Breads 25 – 43

BLUEBERRY TEA BREAD	33
BRAN DINNER ROLLS	27
BROWN BREAD	26
BUTTERHORNS	29
CARAMEL PECAN ROLLS	42
CINNAMON FLOP COFFEE CAKE	41
CINNAMON ROLLS	43
CREAM-FILLED COFFEE CAKE	39
"DIABETIC" RAISIN BRAN MUFFINS	36
DOUGHNUTS -- I	38
DOUGHNUTS -- II	38
ENGLISH MUFFINS IN A LOAF	37
EXCELLENT COATING	25
FRENCH BREAD	25
FRUIT AND CHEESE BREAD	32
FRUIT SWIRL COFFEE CAKE	40
MA'S QUICK BANANA BREAD	33
MUFFINS	35

Breads, cont.

OVERNIGHT ROLLS	28
PUMPKIN CHEESE BREAD	34
QUICK MINCEMEAT COFFEE CAKE	41
RYE BREAD	30
SOFT PRETZELS	30
STRAWBERRY BREAD	31
SUPER PANCAKES	35

Cakes 63 - 79

ANGEL FOOD CAKE	63
APPLE CAKE	74
BANANA CAKE	78
BANANA TOPSY TURVY CAKE	66
CHOCOLATE SHEET CAKE	63
COWBOY CAKE	64
CRUMB CAKE	64
FRUIT COCKTAIL CAKE -- I	68

Cakes, cont.

FRUIT COCKTAIL CAKE -- II	69
GINGERBREAD DELUXE	67
HEAVENLY WHITE CAKE	76
HOT FUDGE PUDDING CAKE	79
MOM'S APPLE CAKE	70
OATMEAL CAKE	73
PINEAPPLE CAKE	77
PINEAPPLE UPSIDE DOWN CAKE	75
RHUBARB CAKE	65
SALAD DRESSING CAKE	69
SPICE CAKE	77
TURTLE CAKE	71
ZUCCHINI CAKE	72

Cookies   80 - 101

ANDY'S COOKIES	90
APPLE BROWNIES	82

Cookies, cont.

APPLE PIE BARS	85
BROWNIES	87
BUTTERSCOTCH OATMEAL COOKIES	101
CHOCO-BUTTERSCOTCH BARS	80
CHOCOLATE CHIP BROWNIES	84
CHOCOLATE CHIP CREAM CHEESE BARS	80
CHOCOLATE CHIP OATMEAL COOKIES	91
CHRISTMAS COOKIES	89
COCONUT OATMEAL COOKIES	94
CREAM CHEESE BARS	87
FAVORITE CHOCOLATE CHIP COOKIES	92
GINGER COOKIES	96
LEMON CHEESE BARS	83
MINCEMEAT-FILLED BARS	81
MOM'S OATMEAL COOKIES	91
MONSTER COOKIES	97
PEPPERNUTS	88

Cookies, cont.

PUFF COOKIES 98

PUMPKIN BARS 86

PUMPKIN COOKIES 93

7 - LAYER BARS 84

SQUASH OR PUMPKIN COOKIES . . . 96

SUGAR COOKIES 92

SWEDISH CREAM WAFERS 99

WHOOPIE PIES 100

WORLD'S BEST SUGAR COOKIES . . . 95

ZUCCHINI DROP COOKIES 95

Desserts   102 - 115

APPLE CINNAMON PUFFS 111

APPLE CRISP -- I 112

APPLE CRISP -- II 112

APPLE DESSERT. 107

BLUEBERRY CHEESE CAKE 106

Desserts, cont.

BREAD PUDDING -- I	114
BREAD PUDDING -- II	114
BUTTER BRICKLE & PEACH DESSERT	113
CAKE DESSERT	106
CINNAMON PUDDING	113
CROW NEST PUDDING	108
DATE PUDDING	102
FRUIT PIZZA -- I	104
FRUIT PIZZA -- II	105
ICE CREAM ROLL	110
PEACH CRISP GOOD DESSERT	115
PUMPKIN CAKE ROLL	109
STRAWBERRY TRIFLE	103

House Recipes   15 - 24

BIG BRAN MUFFINS	16
BLUEBERRY MUFFINS	16

House Recipes, cont.

CREAM CHEESE BROWNIES	23
CUSTARD PIE	20
LEMON BARS	22
OATMEAL PIE	20
PEANUT BUTTER BARS	21
PECAN PIE	17
PINEAPPLE COOKIES	19
PUMPKIN PIE	18
RHUBARB CUSTARD PIE	18
WHITE BREAD	15
ZUCCHINI BARS	24

Pies   44 - 62

APPLE PIE -- I	48
APPLE PIE -- II	49
CARAMEL CREAM PIE	54
CHOCOLATE CHIFFON PIE	47

Pies, cont.

CUSTARD PIE	51
FRESH FRUIT PIES	46
LEMON CAKE PIE	53
MINCEMEAT	62
OATMEAL PIE -- I	57
OATMEAL PIE -- II	57
OLD FASHIONED SUGAR CREAM PIE	51
PEACH ICE CREAM PIE	61
PIE CRUST -- I	44
PIE CRUST -- II	44
PIE CRUST -- III	45
PINEAPPLE CREAM PIE	55
PUMPKIN CHIFFON PIE	60
PUMPKIN CUSTARD PIE	50
PUMPKIN GINGERSNAP PIE	59
PUMPKIN PIE	49
RASPBERRY-PEAR PIE	52

Pies, cont.

RHUBARB PIE DELIGHT 47

SNOW GHOST PIE 54

SOUR CREAM LEMON PIE 53

SOUR CREAM RAISIN PIE 58

VANILLA CRUMB PIE 56

NOTES

FOR INFORMATION

About ordering additional copies of
Buggy Wheel Restaurant Cookbook, Vol. II,
Pies, Breads & Baked Desserts (ISBN 0-927644-14-2)

About ordering copies of
Buggy Wheel Restaurant Cookbook, Vol. I,
Main Dishes & Vegetables (ISBN 0-927644-06-1)

About additional volumes in the series

RETURN THE COUPON for information or call

(219) 768-4444

Buggy Wheel Restaurant
P.O. Box 353
Shipshewana, IN 46565

- -

Send information:
__ Buggy Wheel Cookbook, Vol.I: Main Dishes & Vegetables
__ Buggy Wheel Cookbook, Vol.II: Pies, Breads & Baked Desserts
__ other cookbooks in the series
__ bakery products from the Bread Box Bake Shop

Mail to: Buggy Wheel Restaurant
           P.O. Box 353
           Shipshewana, IN 46565

Name _____

Address _____

City _____ ST _____ ZIP _____

- -

USE COUPON ON REVERSE SIDE
To Request Information on Ordering
Additional Copies of This Book
and Other Cookbooks in the Series